PUB WALKS
IN
The Chilterns

THIRTY CIRCULAR WALKS
AROUND CHILTERNS INNS

Alan Charles

COUNTRYSIDE BOOKS
NEWBURY, BERKSHIRE

COUNTRYSIDE BOOKS
3 Catherine Road
Newbury, Berkshire

ISBN 1 85306 180 8

Cover illustration by Colin Doggett
Photographs and maps by the author

Produced through MRM Associates Ltd., Reading
Typeset by Paragon Typesetters, Sandycroft, Chester
Printed in England by J. W. Arrowsmith Ltd., Bristol

Contents

MAP SYMBOLS

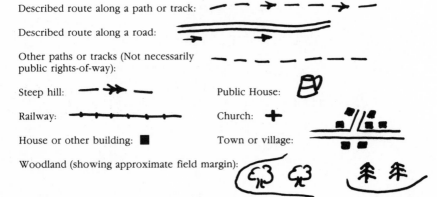

Introduction

Gone are the days when the typical village pub was likely to be basic and unadorned, where the hardiest and least demanding of walkers could be found, and where the menu was limited to pork pies, peanuts and crisps. While there are some who regret the passing, I think most now welcome the newer breed of pub where a good meal can be enjoyed in pleasant, comfortable surroundings.

Licensees often help this along by maintaining an old-world atmosphere in their pubs, keeping what is best from the past while refurbishing in traditional style. Add to this the almost universal support for 'real ale', and today's village pub has just about all the walker could want (apart from good health and good weather!) when setting foot in the countryside.

Many of the pubs described in this book were recommended by friends and acquaintances – mostly for the quality of the food. Others were discovered by chance. Selecting 30 pubs from the long list of suggestions and discoveries was a difficult task, but one made easier by the simple matter of their location. It was necessary for each pub to be on the route of an enjoyable circular walk of about 4 miles in length and for the whole collection of walks to be well spread out across the Chilterns – from the Dunstable Downs in the north to the Thames in the south. Some otherwise excellent pubs were excluded because a suitable walk could not be woven around them, or because they were too near other good pubs.

In spite of the relaxation in licensing laws, many pubs keep more or less to the traditional opening hours. Give or take ½ hour at each end, these are 11.30 am to 2.30 pm and 6 pm to 11 pm Monday-Saturday, with Sunday restricted by law to 12 noon-3 pm and 7 pm-10.30 pm. I have referred to these as 'normal' hours, mentioning actual times only when they differ significantly from the average. Meals are usually available between 12 noon and 2 pm-2.30 pm. The evening 'sittings' vary widely, the most popular being 7 pm-9.30 pm. Sunday is often cook's night off, and there may be other times when food is not available or when the choice is limited. Details of these variations are given in each chapter.

You may be one of the many walkers who like to carry their own food and eat this at a pub. Some licencees are happy with this, and I have indicated who they are. It goes without saying that you would be expected to buy drinks from the bar and to eat your food in the garden. Before taking advantage of this do please check with the licensee, especially if you are leading a party. You can well imagine the impact of 10 or 20 ramblers in a small beer garden – all eating DIY and leaving little room for less self-sufficient customers! Some licensees strongly oppose the practice of customers eating their own food on the premises, be it only in the garden, so to avoid confrontation it is well worth making absolutely certain about this before tucking into those sandwiches.

Most of the pubs in this book have their own car parks, and most licensees are happy for you to leave your car there while you are on the walk. If you intend to do this, do please mention the fact to the licensee. A solitary car left in an otherwise empty car park could cause some concern.

Bus services are given only where their frequency is two-hourly or better. Routes and timings can change at short notice, so it is a good idea to check with the appropriate operating company before deciding on a walk. Addresses and phone numbers for timetable enquiries are given at the end of the book.

If you have a dog, he would doubtless love to come with you on these walks, so I have indicated where in each pub he can be taken. This is usually limited to the public bar or the garden, often to the garden only. If it's been a muddy walk it would be right and proper to ensure that his feet are clean before allowing him across the threshold. The same applies to us humans. In most pubs, muddy boots or shoes are definitely not welcome, and their presence can only damage the good reputation that walkers generally have. The solution is to carry a spare pair of shoes – or dine in your socks!

The walks average about 4 miles in length and should take two-two and a half hours to complete. They are all along public rights of way or permissive paths.

Two of the 1:50 000 Landranger series Ordnance Survey maps together cover most of the walks. These are sheets 165 (Aylesbury and Leighton Buzzard) and 175 (Reading and Windsor). Of the remaining walks, three are covered by sheet 166 (Luton and Hertford) and two by sheet 176 (North-West London). These maps are invaluable because they are on a scale useful to walkers, and because they include footpaths and bridleways. Another excellent source of reference is the series of 20 footpath maps published by the Chiltern Society. These maps are good value for money and can be purchased from numerous outlets – from large bookshops to small newsagents. And they even include the names of pubs!

6

As you get into the walks you can hardly fail to notice the liberal use of compass bearings. These are given where the paths are not as clearly marked as you would wish, or where they might in future become so. While some of the features that now help to define the route – hedges, woods, barns, signposts etc – might disappear at the whim of man, compass bearings stay more or less exactly as they are. If young children are walking with you, there is an added benefit in carrying a compass. Hand it over to them and they will be occupied for the duration of the walk!

Alan Charles
Spring 1992

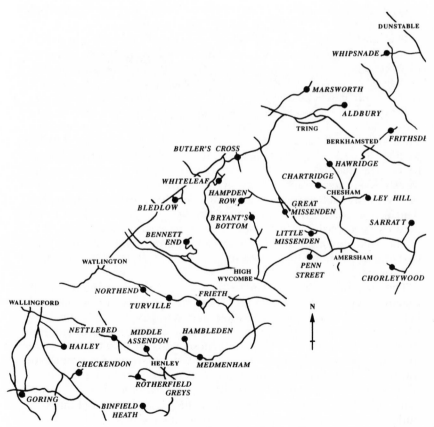

Area map shows locations of the walks.

Whipsnade
The Old Hunters Lodge

The Old Hunters Lodge makes a very pretty picture, with its thatched roofs, its timber framing, and its beautifully kept gardens. Much of the 'Lodge' is of modern construction, but in traditional style and matching the original, central part. The original bar area is still there; and since the bar itself is now in the adjacent lounge, this tiny room is suitable for families – but only two small families! The lounge is a complete contrast: it has a settee, armchairs, and a grand piano.

There is a good choice of very reasonably priced meals from the bar menu, including fish dishes, steak and mushroom pie, sirloin steak, sandwiches, salads and ploughman's. If you prefer something a little more 'upmarket' the restaurant is the place to be – with beautifully arranged dining tables, and a menu that is something to write home about. Restaurant and bar meals are served every day: 11.30 am-2.30 pm and 6 pm-10 pm Monday-Saturday, 12 noon-2 pm and 7 pm-10 pm on Sundays. If you like real ale, Greene King Abbot Ale and IPA are available. There is no draught cider, unfortunately.

Dogs are welcome, but only if under close control.

Telephone: Whipsnade (0582) 872228.

How to get there: The pub is on the B4540 close to its junction with the B4541 2½ miles south of Dunstable. Luton and District bus 43/245 from Luton, Dunstable and Hemel Hempstead bus station, calls here approximately every two hours Monday-Saturday.

Parking: At the pub, or in the small (free) car park by the B4540/4541 junction nearby.

Length of the walk: 4¼ miles. OS Map Landranger series 166 Luton and Hertford (GR 014181). A very small part of the walk is included on the Chiltern Society Footpath Map No. 19.

A walk to suit most sorts and conditions – perhaps even the children. Without too much climbing it places you on the heights of Dunstable Downs, with its gliders, kites and ice cream. For the more serious-minded there are the beautifully reinstated Kensworth chalk quarries (a Site of Special Scientific Interest), the Information Centre on Dunstable Downs (open daily except Mondays) and the Whipsnade Tree Cathedral. Whipsnade Zoo? – that must wait for another day!

The Walk

From the Old Hunters Lodge go left along the B4540 and over the road crossing to a small car park on the left (where you may have parked your car). Pass to the left of a board showing a map and a circular 'way walk' across Whipsnade Heath and leave the car park through a horse barrier on the 'tree side'. When the path divides after a few yards take the right-hand branch (90°) and, passing a seat on the left, go straight on over a crossing-path and under the trees. When you meet another crossing-path later on, continue forward – with the yellow arrow – through a horse barrier and along the right-hand edge of a field, between a wire fence and a tall hedge. From the stile at the end of the field go half-left across another field towards a modern house and a road.

Turn right in the road and left over a stile after 50 yards, beyond farm buildings. A short path terminates at a stile on the left, from where you should turn right into a farm track. When the track leads you across a cattle grid turn half-right immediately (40°) across a field to a footpath signpost. Then follow a hedge downhill and rejoin that self-same track. Cross a stile that's tucked away near a solitary barn, then pass to the right of the barn to another stile and go forward along a field-edge.

At the lowest level of the fields, cross a stile in the fence on the left and follow the direction of the yellow arrow uphill to a signpost by an electricity pole (0° – North). That's 150 yards and 'clipping' a hedge corner on the way. Cross the stile here and walk the hillside

9

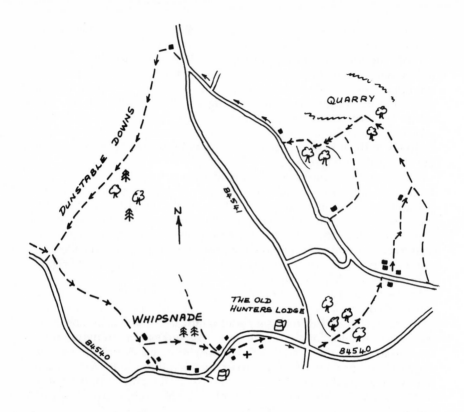

(350°) to another stile at a wood-edge. The path veers left through the wood, passes an old brick shed and comes out into a field — where there's an impressive view of the quarry faces and fields returned to nature and to agriculture.

Turn left here and walk between a hedge and a line of trees (250°) until the path turns left, but now as a private farm track. Go through a waymarked gap on the right here and forward again along the left-hand edge of a field. Stay with the hedge as it progresses uphill, curves right and is replaced by woodland. When you are very nearly at the top of the hill go half-left into a path (260°) under dense bushes — but not before looking back at the recycled quarries. You will soon be along the edge of a field and joining a road at the far end, with a communication tower nearby.

Turn right in the road (Isle of Wight Lane) and walk the unavoidable but quiet ½ mile to the B4541 and that popular weekend retreat, the Dunstable Downs. Turn right in the B4541 and cross to the building opposite – refreshment kiosk, toilets, and an excellent information room.

From the information room drop downhill across the grass (260°) to a solitary waymark post (not to the gate), then bear left and follow the upper edge of the scrub (210°). You will pass a yellow waymark arrow before continuing forward along a well-used path through the scrub. Go over a crossing-path and through a gate at the end of the scrub and straight on in a *very* long field. Beyond the gate placed centrally at the end of this field, a short path (40 yards) will place you beside a stile and a dog gate.

Turn left here into a level path (no need to go forward to the fingerpost) and left again after 30 yards (ie not straight on to a car park) and follow the uphill path between trees and scrub (120°) along with the blue arrows. After following the short left hand end of a pasture this evolves into a good path between hedges. When you eventually arrive at a sturdy metal signpost beyond a new bungalow, turn left to a stile (there is a National Trust sign here) and proceed along the right-hand edge of a field.

From the field's far right-hand corner you should go half-left for a few yards then forward again (80°) alongside the National Trust's Tree Cathedral. There is information about it here and at the main entrance gate, also some log 'pews' on which to rest and gather strength! From the entrance gate (keep well right for this) go forward through a small car park and turn left into a side road, then left into the B4540. Rather than walk along the B4540 you could cross to the green opposite and make your way back to the Old Hunters Lodge, keeping the road in sight.

Marsworth
The White Lion

You could hardly find a pub in a more lively position – right beside the Grand Union Canal along one of its most interesting stretches. The pub's garden takes full advantage of this in its situation alongside the canal. If the weather makes sitting out an unattractive proposition, there are comfortable alternatives in the form of the Canal Bar and the Barn Bar. The Barn Bar does not have a bar as such and is therefore suitable for children.

If there's something the licensee is particularly proud of, it's the home-made pies – all eight varieties. Runners-up in the variety league are the six fish dishes, six kinds of salad, seven sandwich fillings, and four jacket potato fillings. The kitchen is in action every day lunchtimes and evenings, and there is a full choice of meals throughout. This is a free house and offers four real ales – Greene King IPA, Abbot Ale and Rayments Special; also Palmers IPA.

Telephone: Tring (044 282) 2325.

How to get there: The pub is on the B489 (Lower Icknield Way) where it crosses the Grand Union Canal 2 miles north of Tring. Bus 61 from Luton to Aylesbury via Tring calls here one to two hourly Monday-Saturday, two hourly Sunday pm only. NB: Tring station (Euston line) is 1½ miles from Tring.

Parking: In the pub car park or in the British Waterways Board car park opposite.

Length of the walk: 3 miles. OS Map Landranger series 165 Aylesbury and Leighton Buzzard (GR 919142). Chiltern Society Footpath Map No. 18.

An ideal walk for anyone interested in canals or birds, or in an easy-going waterside amble. It includes the towpath of the Grand Union Canal and one of its branches – the delightful Wendover Arm; also the banks of reservoirs that feed these canals. Two optional extensions are proposed: to the Bulbourne Workshops and to the junction with the Aylesbury Arm. Each extension adds an extra ½ mile to the walk, making a grand total of 4 miles.

The Walk
Join the canal towpath by crossing the road from the White Lion public house. The lock just here is one of seven along the next ¾ mile stretch, taking the canal up to its summit level. Each one of these locks has a pair of side ponds, which were part of an ingenious system for saving precious water. Since it took twice as long to get a boat through a lock, this arrangement became unpopular and went out of use.

You will soon have Startopsend and Marsworth reservoirs on your right, where there is a choice between walking along their banks or staying on the towpath. These reservoirs are two of the four hereabouts built with the express purpose of storing water for the canal.

The end of that ¾ mile stretch is marked by an unusual canal feature – a fingerpost giving directions and distances. So now you know that the Grand Union Canal from Braunston in Northamptonshire to Brentford in Middlesex is 93½ miles in length! And that's how it's been since it was opened in 1800, when it was known as the Grand Junction Canal. Because the canal was so successful its locks were doubled to their present width, allowing two boats to pass simultaneously. The long shed adjacent to the fingerpost stands on one of the original single-width locks. This now functions as a dry dock for the maintenance and modification of boats.

For the main walk your next move is to cross the little bridge here

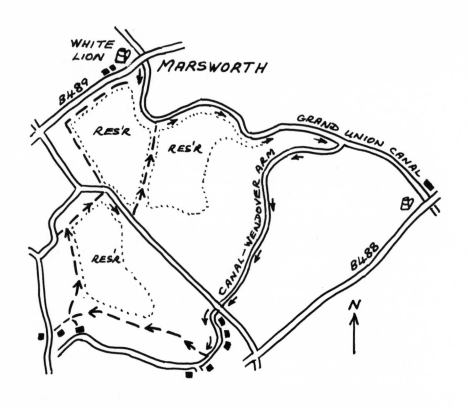

and double back to the towpath of the Wendover Arm, but by staying in the main canal you would, after ¼ mile or so, arrive opposite the Bulbourne Workshops. In addition to being in an attractive building, these workshops are vital to the canal network, for it is here that replacement lock gates – which last only 25-30 years – are constructed.

Back at the little bridge and walking along the delightful Wendover Arm, you have directly ahead a view of the hillside of Tring Park and, to the right of this, Aston Hill above Halton. It is from under these and other hills that spring water flows. This is collected by the reservoirs via feeder channels and then pumped into the Wendover Arm. From the Wendover Arm it flows into the main canal at summit level – replacing the 50,000 gallons 'lost' by each passing boat!

From the road bridge at New Mills the towpath changes sides. At the second bend in the canal and very nearly opposite the mill's circular metal silos, leave the canal for a path crossing the field on the right

(250°). The path heads towards a shallow dip and meets another path coming in from the right – also crossing the field. Go left in a track after a few yards, cross a ditch and turn immediately right. With a field on the left and the ditch on the right, follow the meandering path under trees until you come out into a clearing. Walk under the line of tall chestnut trees here (260°) along a wide grassy path, with a reservoir in view well over to the right and a pumping station 100 yards away on the left.

Now don't cross the stile ahead – leading onto the pumping station's drive – but turn right (10°). This will take you to the right of a wired enclosure and into a path under young chestnut trees. A short distance along the path an opening on the right (and a hide soon after that) gives an out-of-this-world view across the shallows of the reservoir. The ducks, the geese and the birds clearly feel at home here.

Ignore a branch on the right as you continue forward under the trees. When your path eventually turns right stay with it into the open, with the reservoir still on your right and the tall chimneys of Pitstone cement works directly ahead. Walk along the wall of the reservoir and go right in the road from the far left-hand corner (150°). When you are just beyond the limit of the reservoir cross the road to a stile and gate opposite, doubling back momentarily and soon passing a 'Coarse Fishing' notice. It's now a short amble along the causeway between Startopsend and Marsworth reservoirs back to the Grand Union Canal. With all the wild life hereabouts, it comes as no surprise that these reservoirs, in addition to their utilitarian function, have the status of National Nature Reserve.

Turning left into the Grand Union, you will soon be back at the White Lion. Before going inside you could continue for a further ¼ mile to the Aylesbury Arm of the canal. The original plan to take this branch as far as Abingdon and to link it with the Oxford Canal, did not materialise. It has seen very little traffic since the end of the 19th century, and in 1964 plans were afoot to close it altogether. The Aylesbury Canal Society came to the rescue and its future is now secure.

Aldbury
The Greyhound

If there's something The Greyhound and the village of Aldbury have in common, it's their popularity with walkers and visitors. This comes as no surprise: the village with its unspoilt cottages, its church and its pond; The Greyhound with its welcome, its comfort and its excellent food. The pub has four rooms where you can eat and drink, including the public bar with its magnificent fireplace and old-world atmosphere. You may take your children into the restaurant (if having meals) and your dog into the public bar. If you have dog *and* children, then you have a problem!

The entire menu fits onto the blackboard, but there is a very good choice and that choice is frequently varied. Except for Monday evenings, you can enjoy a meal from a full menu any lunchtime or evening. The pub is open for drinking 'all day' Saturday (11 am-11 pm) all the year round; on other days the hours are 'normal'. Real ales are Benskins Best Bitter and Young's PA.

Telephone: Aldbury Common (044 285) 228.

How to get there: The pub is near Aldbury church and the village pond, 2½ miles from Tring along Station Road (Tring station). The walk passes within ¼ mile of the station, so if you are coming by train you could join the walk by turning right out of the station and following the right-hand sweep of the road until it turns sharp left; then take your cue from page 19. Trains to Tring station from London (Euston) run half hourly Monday-Saturday, hourly Sunday. Bus 27 runs one to two hourly between Tring (Rose & Crown) and Aldbury via Tring station Monday-Saturday only.

Parking: The Greyhound does not have its own car park, but there is a public parking area at the front. There is also a car park on the recreation ground a short distance along the Ivinghoe road. You could start the walk from there, since it passes that way.

Length of the walk: 4 miles. OS Map Landranger series 165 Aylesbury and Leighton Buzzard (GR 965125). Chiltern Society Footpath Map No. 19.

This is an easy walk in which you can enjoy the hills without the climbing! The wooded hillside of Ashridge and the bare slopes of Pitstone Hill are particularly impressive, and beech-clad Aldbury Nower is a delight – as is the Ridgeway Path that passes through it.

The Walk

From The Greyhound go left in the road and walk along this for less than ¼ mile to a bridleway on the left just beyond the recreation ground. Ignore the first stile on the right (by an iron gate) along the bridleway and continue to the next, where there is a footpath/ bridleway signpost. This is ⅓ mile from the road. Turn right here along a hedge-lined path (320°).

This will lead you between fields to another stile, then onto a golf course and straight on along the right hand side of a hedge. Aldbury Nower Wood will be in view directly ahead.

When you are three-quarters of the way along this piece of golf course, go left through a gap and along the right hand side of another hedge (240°). Turn right a short distance beyond a venerable oak tree and follow the waymarks all the way up to a pedestrians' gate in the furthest left-hand corner of Aldbury Nower Wood (290° from the oak tree). Going straight on through the wood you will

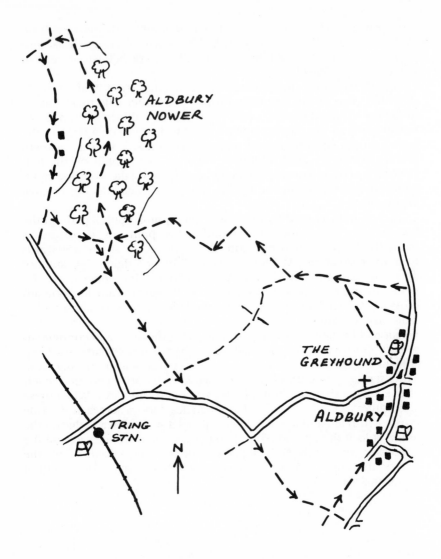

meet the Ridgeway long distance path, identified by an acorn waymark. Turn right into this and ascend a double flight of steps almost immediately. The fence on the left encloses an area of land managed by the Herts and Middlesex Wildlife Trust, who maintain it as a grassland habitat for chalk-loving flowers and butterflies.

Continue in the path – mostly under trees and guided by the

Ridgeway acorns – for more than ½ mile until a stile places you on the open grassland of Pitstone Hill. The town of Tring comes into view on the far side of the Bulbourne valley, as does Pitstone cement works directly ahead.

Turn left almost immediately beyond the stile. Walk steeply downhill clear of the hawthorn bushes to another stile tucked away in the far left-hand corner. Cross the stile and walk straight on down for 50 yards to yet another stile on the left, just before a bend in the path and opposite a large chalk quarry. From the stile walk a level path under tall trees – with Aldbury Nower in view uphill on the left. Beyond a stile at Northfield Grange a drive will take you in a right-hand curve away from the house, but soon back into the original alignment.

After ¼ mile along the drive you should join an uphill path on the left running just inside the wood. This point of departure is immediately beyond an iron gate in the drive and about 150 yards from the road ahead. At a fork in the path branch right (170° and not up to the gate in view ahead) and soon follow the upper edge of a field. Beyond this you will again meet the Ridgeway Path at a footpath crossing. Go straight on here along the level path, once again with a field on the right.

Ignore a bridleway crossing ⅓ mile along this path and continue to a road. Go forward in the road and, when it turns sharp left, keep straight on by joining a bridleway (along with those arriving from Tring station — see 'How to get there' section). Ignore a path on the left after a few yards and follow a hedge and overhead wires. When these wires intersect with others at right-angles (not where a horse-ride crosses) turn left and join a field-edge from a stile, with a hedge on the left. A stile at the far end of the hedge leads into a cul-de-sac, and the cul-de-sac into Trooper Road. You will find the village pond, the stocks, and The Greyhound pub when you have walked the length of Trooper Road.

Frithsden
The Alford Arms

What once made the Alford Arms especially interesting was that it brewed its own beer. Alongside the pub a low building housed the equipment where four varieties were produced. One of these – Pickled Squirrel – found its way into the Beef and Squirrel Pie. No doubt many customers would be delighted if 'home brew' at the Alford Arms could be revived.

In addition to the regular menu, up to five 'specials' are on offer every lunchtime and evening. This includes Sundays – when you can alternatively enjoy a traditional lunch. It is all good quality food, and nicely presented. There are four real ales: Flowers Original and IPA, Boddingtons Best Bitter and Castle Eden. If cider is preferred there are bottled versions or draught Strongbow Dry. Drinking times at the Alford Arms are the maximum possible: 11 am-11 pm Monday-Saturday, 12 noon-3 pm and 7 pm-10.30 pm on Sunday.

Since the pub is situated in a quiet rural setting, the garden – which is at the front – is little disturbed by passing traffic. If your dog is with you, he can share in the pleasure. He can also be taken into the Top Bar, a privilege which the law of the land doesn't grant to children unless they are over 14.

Telephone: Hemel Hempstead (0442) 864480.

How to get there: The pub is 2 miles north-east of Berkhamsted. Take the White Hill road by Berkhamsted Castle and follow the road signs to Frithsden.

Parking: In the pub's own car park. Roadside parking is minimal.

Length of the walk: 3¾ miles. OS Map Landranger series 166 Luton and Hertford (GR 017098). Chiltern Society Footpath Map No. 20.

The walk dips into three lovely Hertfordshire valleys – at Frithsden, Nettleden and Great Gaddesden. Frithsden and Nettleden are enhanced by well-kept cottages and gardens, Great Gaddesden by its church and by the meandering river Gade. Not surprisingly, these three valleys equate with three fairly steep hills. These are either 'demanding' or 'stimulating', depending on how you see them!

The Walk

Join the 'No Through Road' on the left side of the pub and, passing ornate and beautifully kept Little Manor, go uphill under the trees. This road becomes a rough track before the summit and gives some fine views, including Ashridge House (when viewed from a trio of iron gates on the left). Ignore two stiles on the left (by the third iron gate) and continue forward 60 yards to a horse barrier on the right – just before the track plunges steeply in a cutting. Although traditionally called 'Roman Road', there is no evidence that this track was cut by the Romans. Its other name, 'Spooky Lane', seems more appropriate at this point! The bridge over the cutting was built to carry a drive to Ashridge House.

Go through the barrier, then over a stile and downhill under trees parallel to the track. The path comes out by Nettleden Farm (a bungalow) from where it's a short distance down to a road junction.

There are some nice cottages to see before going left in the road and joining a path on the right after 15 yards (where two signposts disagree about the distance to Great Gaddesden). Walk uphill alongside a very large field, followed by a smaller field and the grounds of a Buddhist Centre – where you cannot fail to notice the 'Stupa', a Buddhist shrine in the middle of the smaller field.

Having reached the road by the entrance to the Buddhist Centre, turn left and cross to a path on the right after 35 yards. Go over the stile here and follow a wood-edge (110°) to another stile at the end of the wood. Then make your way straight on and downhill across a large rough pasture to a hedge-gap beneath a wooden electricity pole (90°), which may be obscured by a stand of hawthorn trees.

Gaddesden Place on the opposite hilltop is looking at you across the Gade valley and should be slightly right as you proceed. From that hedge-gap cross the next pasture towards the right-hand extremity of Great Gaddesden's churchyard trees (130°). Go over the stile here and into the churchyard, where a diversion into the church itself is worthwhile. The nave roof is particularly interesting, as are the carved wooden angels holding it aloft.

Continue down to the churchyard lychgate and turn right by the school. Cross the road to a narrow footpath (signposted to Water End) opposite the Cock and Bottle. The path runs parallel to a private drive before linking up with the left-hand edge of a field. This leads into another field and to a pair of stiles in the far left-hand corner. Although the next move is to turn right, you might like to continue ahead to the river Gade – a short but very pleasant diversion.

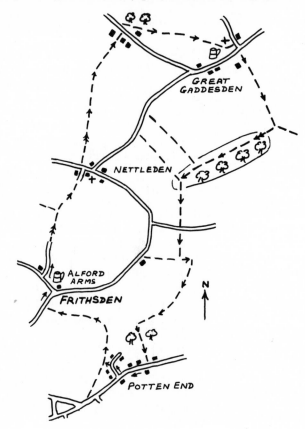

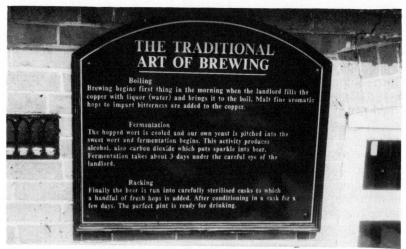

The Alford Arms once brewed its own beer – this plaque explains the procedure.

From that pair of stiles go uphill between a field and a hedge (with Gaddesden Place in view directly behind), then into a long steady climb just inside a wood – all straight on. Ignore all branches until you are 'over the top', that is where the hill begins to descend noticeably and where there is an abundance of holly bushes. At the waymarked divide just here take the left-hand branch (180°). So that you may be certain of your position, the right-hand branch enters a sloping field with a view overlooking a valley. This should not be confused with an earlier branch, which is also into a field – but without the view!

There is another dividing of the ways quite soon (50 yards). Take the right-hand branch to a stile and downhill across a field to a road (180°). Cross to the stile opposite and go slightly right of 'straight on' (200°) to a waymark post and water point in the middle of the fields. Turn left here (140°) and head towards a hedge-corner (where a gap opens to another field); then turn right to follow the curving hedge (hedge left and field right). This will take you up to a stile in the far corner, and under trees alongside the next field. From the next stile turn left and go straight on uphill – soon passing houses on the right – to the road opposite Potten End Farm.

Turn right in the road and, later, right again into Browns Spring, a 'No Through Road' opposite a motor garage. When Browns Spring turns right, keep forward, but now in a footpath and down to a T-junction. Turn right here and stay in the wide shady path as it curves anticlockwise, eventually meeting the road at Frithsden. Go right in the road and first left for the Alford Arms.

Hawridge
The Rose and Crown

This is an ideal pub for anyone with a liking for real ale, since it offers at least six varieties. The draught cider is good too – Addlestones and Stowford Press. Inside, the pub has a comfortable relaxed atmosphere, with separate bar and dining areas. The food is excellent, with an impressive variety of both familiar and unusual items and a choice of about five vegetarian dishes. If you have a hearty appetite you can go on to such delights as the home-made treacle tart, rhubarb crumble or bread and butter pudding – to name but a few! Meals are available every lunchtime (12 noon-2 pm), evenings Monday-Saturday only (7 pm-9 pm). Drinking hours are 'normal'. Although the Rose and Crown does not have a 'no smoking' area, if you require an ash tray on your dining table you will need to ask for one: a silent but polite message to smokers!

Children are welcome in the dining area or in the garden. Dogs may be taken into the bar only, if kept on a lead.

Telephone: Hawridge (0494) 758386.

How to get there: The pub is on a comparatively quiet road 3 miles north of Chesham. The approach from Chesham is via Berkhamsted Road and Vale Road.

Parking: There are two large car parks, one each side of the pub, and limited roadside parking.

Length of the walk: 3½ miles. OS Map Landranger series 165 Aylesbury and Leighton Buzzard (GR 948062). Chiltern Society Footpath Map No. 8.

An easy walk that encompasses the lovely semi-wooded expanse of Hawridge and Cholesbury Commons and one of the most beautiful valleys in the Chilterns. Cholesbury is especially interesting – for its houses, its windmill, and its cricket!

The Walk

With your back to the Rose and Crown's front door (the one that's no longer in use) go left in the road and join a path leaving from the left a few yards before the first road junction (where a sign points to Hawridge Court and church). This will lead you downhill under trees to an attractive settlement of converted farm buildings (Vale Farm) at a road junction. Keep left here – in the Cholesbury road – and, passing a converted barn on the right, soon join a level track ahead. Going forward in this you will notice Willow Tree Cottage on the right after a few hundred yards.

I am taking you along this level route in the valley bottom all the way to Cholesbury Common because it is easy to define. Since horses also come this way you may find this agreeable bridleway less agreeable after wet weather, in which case you would do well to divert uphill on the left at the earliest opportunity. Any clear path through the bracken will do, but you must keep the valley bottom in range if not in sight if you are to avoid the road at the top.

Where the bridleway meets a quiet lane ahead, you should go left for 15 yards or so (*right* if you have been following a higher route) then continue forward in the valley bottom. There is soon another opportunity to follow a higher route – where the views are better, incidentally.

When the bottom bridleway eventually starts to curve left (and uphill) you should say goodbye to it and take the half-left grassy path uphill (280°). If there's cricket on the green at Cholesbury, the sound of it will guide you up, but if you miss the path and find yourself on the Wigginton road you will need to double back sharply left across the common.

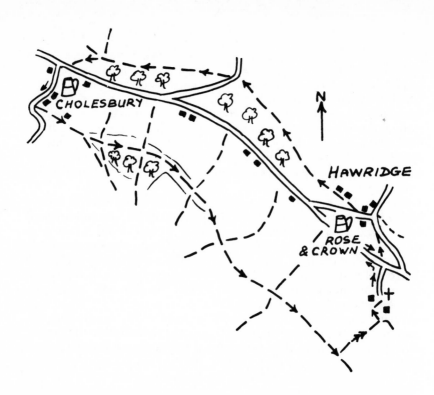

Not far from the Full Moon pub you will find the Bellingdon road, Rays Hill, and after you have walked along this a short distance you will have an excellent view of Cholesbury windmill. This was built in 1884 (replacing an earlier mill) and ended its working life in 1915. It is now a private residence – and its sails are dummies! At the bottom of the hill just before the road turns left you should yourself turn left into a rough drive labelled as a footpath. If you hear the barking of dogs as you pass a painted cottage along this drive, you can rest assured that the sound issues from secure kennels!

Pass to the right of the kennels and cross a stile of sorts into an area of uncultivated land. Ignore a stile on the right quite soon – leading into a wood – and go straight on, with the wood now close on your right. A stile coinciding with the end of the wood will lead you forward into a lovely wild area of trees and scrub, with inconspicuous power lines to guide you through. A beechwood area is next, in the valley floor and exceptionally beautiful in bluebell time. Beyond a strip of younger woodland, a succession of stiles separates sloping fields and leads you straight on along the valley bottom to a hedge-lined bridleway crossing.

26

I suspect that the 'Danger Bull In Field' scrawled on the stile at the crossing, is to deter our kind (I saw nothing!). Go over this stile regardless, and straight on across a meadow, soon following the left edge of a small beechwood. Now taking great care not to become distracted (by conversation or whatever!), you should only proceed along this beechwood for about 250 yards, until you meet a stile at the next field boundary. When over that stile turn left immediately and go uphill towards a break in the trees at the top. A hedge on the left will guide you up, and there's a cattle trough to confirm your direction as you proceed.

Go over a stile in that gap (beside a white gate) and straight on up, with a hedge on the right. This will take you over a stile and forward into a field corner beside another cattle trough, from where you should turn left (not over a stile in the corner). With one eye on a ditch under trees on the right, follow this round to a stile – just before the converted barns of Hawridge Court. The ditch appears to be part of an ancient moated homestead and was cut through when the foundations of the Court were laid.

A narrow path will soon place you in front of the Court, with the church close by. Passing the church on your right, follow the tarmac drive to a T-junction, then turn left for the Rose and Crown.

Chartridge
The Bell

If there's something about The Bell that sets it apart, it is the welcome given to families. It has a children's room that doubles as a games room (video games, pool, etc) and an attractive garden with swings, slides and budgies. Also a bar menu that includes 'meals for young children'. This two page densely-packed menu will also satisfy most, if not all, adult tastes, with delicious and very reasonably priced meals – fish, chicken, grills, steaks, omelettes, salads, vegetarian, etc. The 'Bell Favourites' are an extension to the familiar ploughman's: farmer's (ham), fisherman's (mackerel) and woodman's (sausage).

Meals are normally served Monday to Saturday lunchtimes only. However, if you would like a meal at Sunday lunchtime – for yourself or a party – this can be put in hand by prior arrangement over the telephone. Walkers self-sufficient in food, but buying drinks, should ask before consuming their food in the garden. Real ale at The Bell is Benskins and Burton, with Brakspear Ordinary as 'guest'.

If Fido is walking with you, he will not be out of place here – with Sasha and Sophie, the pub's poodle and labrador, already in residence.

Telephone: Chesham (0494) 782878.

How to get there: The pub is 2 miles north-west of Chesham and can be approached by joining Park Road opposite Chesham's public library. Bus 336/337 runs hourly Monday-Saturday from Watford Junction station (90 minute journey) via Amersham Metropolitan station.

Parking: In the pub's own car park or in the roadside – where space is limited.

Length of the walk: 3 ¾ miles. OS Map Landranger series 165 Aylesbury and Leighton Buzzard (GR 932037). Chiltern Society Footpath Map No. 8.

This walk explores one of those marvellous valleys that radiate from Chesham. It also takes a look at Lee Common, a lovely unspoilt open space. If you have strong feelings about rights-of-way preservation, you could help to keep open a ⅓ mile stretch of difficult path. If you don't, an alternative route is described. This involves a short hill of moderate steepness, one of three such hills along the walk.

The Walk

Go over the stile directly opposite The Bell and make your way to the far right-hand corner of the very large field (240°). Cross the stile here (you will not see it until you are on it) and, as directed by the black 'parish' arrow, go left and left again immediately, placing Cogdales Farm behind you and a hedge on your left. You will pass an old pond on your right as you walk the 70 yards to another stile. From here a black arrow points right directing you downhill (220°) to a stile in the heel of what turns out to be an L-shaped field. From the stile a narrow path drops down to a lane, where you should turn right.

When the lane soon turns left, keep straight on, but now in a bridleway along the valley bottom. Before the bridleway curves left you will go over a crossing-path where an intimidating 'Beware of the Bull' notice is possibly not the only one you have seen today (you may be wondering where on earth he is).

The bridleway eventually skirts the edge of a beechwood on the right, while there's a field on the left. After this the field and beechwood change sides and you will find yourself just inside the wood – and still in the valley bottom.

From the far end of the wood there's ⅓ mile of footpath directly ahead which you are likely to find restricted and overgrown. If you are dressed for the part and have a stick to flail the nettles, you will be doing us all a good turn by helping to keep the path open (a useful task for a large walking party). The path terminates at a rough drive

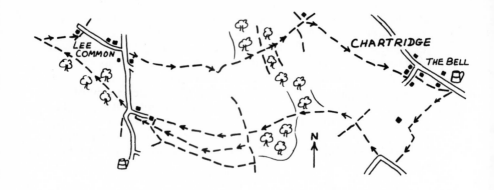

adjacent to an attractive cottage garden. We'll see you there!

For an easier route go left and uphill in the bridleway for about 100 yards (that's half-way up) and turn right into a level bridleway between fields, with trees on the right. When the left-hand field comes to an end, continue forward just inside a wood. Coming out of the wood at a junction of ways, go forward again, but now in a rough drive. The stalwarts who fought their way along the lower path should turn right into the drive.

Turn left at a T-junction in the drive by Rose Cottage and go along to a road. Cross the road to a gate opposite and follow the path straight on through a wood. After almost ½ mile a stile will place you on Lee Common. Turn right here and half-right (80°) after a few yards, climbing the common diagonally to an electricity pole with wires branching three ways. A stile behind this will place you along a field edge leading slightly uphill to a rough drive (Cherry Tree Lane) by Garden Cottage. Turn right in the drive and follow it through to a T-junction, passing houses old and new. At the T-junction cross to a stile opposite, by Evenley House.

You now have for company the right-hand edge of three fields in succession. This is straight on and amounts to ⅓ mile, until you arrive at a stile and iron gate in the dip of the fields. There is a horse trough here (nee cattle trough) and a waymark that bids you turn half-left (45°) to join the right-hand side of a tall hedge. The hedge evolves into a wood-edge and you are led downhill to a stile in the field corner. At the same time a double row of electricity wires has been running parallel to you in the dip of the field well over to your right.

Go over a crossing inside the wood and uphill in a muddy bridleway. There is an escape route running parallel – but the horses have been there before you!

30

The bridleway soon narrows considerably and, after 150 yards, crosses a concreted area. You should ignore a stile on the right here and continue forward a further 50 yards passing a pond on the left; then go over a stile on the right at a footpath crossing. Cross the field here to its far left-hand corner (120° – half-left when your back is to the stile) and go along the edge of the next field under a row of fine oak trees, with fields on both sides. Houses come into view ahead as you continue forward, and the path veers slightly left to a stile. This will lead you along the left edge of a playing field and onto a road from the field's far left-hand corner. Turn left in the road and, for The Bell, right at a T-junction.

Ley Hill
The Swan

When you dine in this lovely old timber-framed pub you may value one of its special features more than any other – the 'no-smoking' dining room. Children may also eat there, as well as in the Snug Room off the public bar (it's as nice as it sounds). The large 'safe family garden' is equipped with children in mind – but not dogs: they are welcome in the public bar only.

The four-page menu card is an attraction in itself, with a wide range of delicious meals listed, including steaks, fish, salads, vegetarian dishes and 'firm favourites' (chicken and asparagus pie, steak and mushroom pie, lasagne, etc). And there are a number of sweets that you may not be able to resist. Children under twelve have their own colourful menu card – where fish fingers are notable by their absence. With the exception of Sunday evenings, meals are served every lunchtime and evening by a happy, friendly staff.

Real ales are Tetley, Benskins, Burton, and Young's Special. Draught cider is Addlestones – a comparative rarity in these parts, and very nice.

Telephone: Chesham (0494) 783075.

How to get there: The pub is 2 miles east of Chesham. Join White Hill from the A416 near Sainsbury's store, Chesham and follow the road signs to Ley Hill. Bus 373 runs hourly from Chesham Broadway Monday-Saturday only. Chesham station is on the Metropolitan Line.

Parking: There is space for parking in front of The Swan and on Ley Hill Common nearby.

Length of the walk: 3½ miles. OS Map Landranger series 165 Aylesbury and Leighton Buzzard (GR 990019). Chiltern Society Footpath Map No. 17.

A nice easy walk that explores the countryside east of Chesham. It enjoys a prospect of the Chess valley as well as a few miles of pleasant Buckinghamshire countryside. A good walk if you wish to make the most of the sunshine (assuming there is some!) since much of the route is out in the open.

The Walk

As you leave The Swan and immediately pass The Crown, look for a signpost on the left pointing to the Methodist church and the War Memorial Institute. If you make your way in that direction you will find a path running between the two buildings. This passes the end of a cul-de-sac and shortly ends at a stile, on the left. From the stile go along the right-hand edge of a field (maintaining your previous direction) to another stile in its far right-hand corner.

Soon after you enter the wood ahead you will be very glad that you brought your compass (if indeed you have), for there are numerous paths criss-crossing the wood – too many to put into words. With this valuable instrument to the fore you should maintain a westerly direction (270°). If you are not thus equipped you should walk more-or-less straight on, keeping to the main path as far as possible. By either method you will eventually be confronted by an array of deep worked-out pits, now a playground for small boys on bicycles.

Making your way carefully to the far side of these pits you should encounter a rail (a stile without a step) in the border between the wood and an irregular field. This is near the right-hand side of the deepest pit and not far from the right-hand extremity of the wood. Now you must cross the field to another rail a little left of the furthest corner. This is due west again (270°). From now on it's easier.

Go straight on across the next (small) field to a stile at a lane, near a terrace of attractive cottages. Turn left in the lane and follow this up to the Five Bells pub – a good quarter-way house! You could alternatively cross the lane to a stile and go left along a field-edge to the pub.

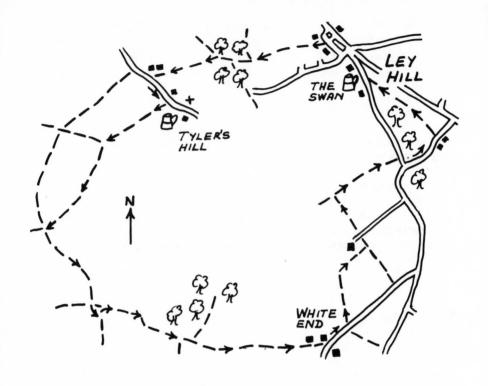

Backstepping a little from the Five Bells you will find a rail just prior to the pub. Cross the field from here to a stile in the opposite corner (260°), near the left-hand end of a rank of trees. Go straight on from there, along the left edge of a field, and when you see a footpath signpost ahead continue forward – in footpath CM49. As you now make your way downhill between fields you have part of the Chess valley in view half-left, confirmed by the sound of 'Met' trains on the Chesham branch.

At the bottom of the hill turn left into the appropriately named Bottom Lane (a bridleway) and follow its curving route for ⅓ mile to a junction of ways. You could go over the stile on the left by the signpost 'CM55 White End' but it might be easier to continue a little further to a crossing in a pronounced S-bend. Take the 'CM29 Green Lane to White End' branch – left and uphill at first and for a total of ¾ mile to a lane at White End Park Farm. Along part of this route a parallel path has been worked just inside Ladies Wood, doubtless to avoid mud.

Turn left in the lane and, passing a pair of cottages on the left (including Cherry Cottage), join the first path on the left after 100 yards, by an iron gate. Walk between fields along the left side of a hedge, with a wire fence left (360°), and go straight on under hawthorn trees at the far end, ignoring a stile on the left. The path soon turns right, still under the trees, and passes an old shed and the immaculate gardens of Meadham's Farm.

When a waymarked stile deposits you in a field turn left (340°) and soon cross the 'farm' drive by means of two more stiles. Keep straight on across the fields (340°) until you meet a wide rough track and turn right.

Turn right into a road after ¼ mile and very soon left into another, signposted to Bovingdon and Hemel Hempstead. Follow this uphill to Ley Hill Common and a footpath signpost opposite the derelict barns of Ashridge Cottage. Looking left across the common you will have the welcome sight of The Swan, and little more than grass to separate you from it.

Sarratt
The Cricketers

The Cricketers is in a delightful setting overlooking Sarratt Green. Surprisingly, cricket cannot be seen from here, the only 'play' being that enjoyed by white ducks on the village pond.

Meals at The Cricketers are good wholesome affairs, nothing too exotic and very reasonably priced – as befits an ordinary but homely village pub. They are served every day 12 noon-2 pm and, with slightly less choice, 6 pm-9 pm Thursday-Saturday. Real ales are Courage Best, Courage Directors, and a guest beer.

You can eat and drink in the comfort of one of the three rooms (while taking stock of an interesting collection of Toby jugs and framed bank notes) or at tables at the front of the pub. Children can join you in the dining room if having meals. Dogs can be taken into the public bar and part of the saloon bar, but not in the dining room.

Telephone: Kings Langley (092 326) 263729.

How to get there: The pub is 5 miles from Watford and 3 miles from junction 18 of the M25. Bus 352 runs from Watford town centre via Croxley Metropolitan and BR stations two hourly Monday-Saturday only.

Parking: Either in The Cricketers own car park or in the cul-de-sac at the front of the pub.

Length of the walk: 4 miles. OS Map Landranger series 166 Luton and Hertford, or 176 North-West London (GR 044992). Chiltern Society Footpath Map No. 5.

This is one of many lovely walks that can be enjoyed in and around the Chess valley. After passing the ancient parish church we descend the valley and meet the river Chess at one of its most beautiful crossings. Following a short traverse of the opposite hillside we recross the river and return to Sarratt. There are two moderately steep hills to climb, but the rewards − in terms of the view − are out of this world!

The Walk

From The Cricketers turn left into a side road just beyond the village pond, then left into a tarmac drive signposted 'Church End ½'. This is just to the right of Ivy Cottage. The drive soon evolves into a rough track alongside houses and terminates at a stile, the stile leading into a field corner. Go forward along the left edge of three-and-a-bit fields in succession to a stile and gate in the far left-hand corner, then forward again along a narrow path under trees. Passing gardens on the left you will soon arrive at a rough drive. Cross this to a kissing-gate opposite. Keep left along the edge of a field for a short distance before striking across the field (ie straight on) towards Sarratt church (180°).

Having arrived at the churchyard gate you may wish to go into the church itself. This pleasure can be reserved until later, since we shall be passing this way again towards the end of the walk.

With your back to the church and the churchyard gate (facing the field and almost doubling back) you should walk alongside a holly hedge (310°) to a iron gate and stile leading into an avenue of trees. Go downhill between the trees and, when these terminate, straight on along the level right-hand edge of a field, with a tall hedge on the right. Stay with the field-edge as it curves left and downhill, and cross a stile in the hedge about a third of the way down. Once over that stile follow the left edge of another field (310°) and join a narrow road from the field's far left-hand corner.

Go left in the lane and soon right by Cakebread Cottage (where I recall delicious teas being served in the days of my youth − by a large homely lady!). Stay in the lane as far as Hillsdown Cottage. When the lane turns right go left into a long concrete farm drive labelled with a Chess Valley Walk signpost. The ford and footbridge at the end of the drive help to make this one of the most delightful crossings of the river Chess.

Join the lane on the opposite side of the river and go along this (the lane) until it curves right. Turn left here into a path, then right after 15 yards and steeply uphill. The replanted woodland on your left as you climb replaces trees severely storm damaged. Near the top of the hill the path under the trees curves right (210°) and meets a stile at the wood-edge. From that stile cross a field to another stile (180°) near a barn in the opposite right-hand corner. Turn left here into a rough track, and after a stile and gate bear right (90°) along the edge of a field, with a wood on the right.

When you reach the next field (through a gap) turn left (70°), leaving the wood behind and following a hedge on the left. Take care to branch half-right (110°) when you are nearly half-way down this field, and head for a stile in its far corner. From that stile turn left to

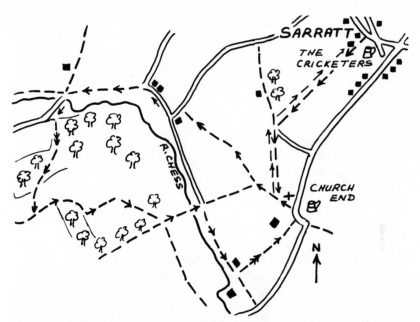

another under trees and cross the valley bottom to a footbridge over the river. Having crossed the bridge turn right and walk parallel to the river, aiming for a stile adjacent to a pair of cottages.

Immediately beyond the cottages go left and uphill, following an iron fence on your left. Goldingtons will be in full view as you climb, and a stile at the top will lead you across a drive and forward to Sarratt church.

Taking the signposted path through the churchyard you will notice, in the walls of the church, natural boulders of Hertfordshire pudding-stone (looking for all the world like pebbles set in concrete) and examples of what are thought to be Roman bricks. Inside the church, what may attract your attention most of all are the beautiful kneelers.

When you have left the churchyard through a kissing-gate and entered a large field, you may recognise the way back to Sarratt. If in doubt you should cross the field diagonally (0° corner to corner) aiming for a point two thirds of the way along a rank of trees (as they appear from this distance), in a path that may not be very evident. From a kissing-gate in the far corner cross a rough drive and join a path backing onto gardens. Straight on now, soon following the right-hand edge of the fields; then along a short drive to Sarratt Green.

Before making a bee-line for The Cricketers, why not walk the length of Sarratt Green, and enjoy its many fine cottages?

Chorleywood
The Stag

A comfortable and beautifully refurbished pub where the polite, welcoming staff prepare and serve a wide range of excellent meals. The regular menu card describes meals with fish (trout, salmon, mackerel, Norfolk crab), a variety of ploughman's, jacket potatoes and baps; also salads and sandwiches. This is supplemented by a long list of 'homecooked specials of the day' chalked on the blackboard. The meals, which are very good value for money, are available every lunchtime and evening except Sunday evening. Children under 14 cannot share the pleasure, except in the garden. Dogs are permitted in the garden only – on a lead.

Real ales include Fullers London Pride and Courage Best, while draught cider is the exceptional Scrumpy Jack.

Telephone: Chorleywood (0923) 282090.

How to get there: The pub is at The Swillet, Chorleywood, less than a mile from junction 17 of the M25. There is a frequent rail service from London (Baker Street and Marylebone); but it's a 1 mile walk from Chorleywood station to The Stag – much of it quite steep.

Parking: In addition to the pub's own car park, there is roadside parking in Stag Lane nearby.

Length of the walk: 4 miles. OS Map Landranger series 176 North-West London (GR 021951). The walk is not covered by a Chiltern Society footpath map.

This easy walk circulates around Newland Park, for many years occupied by a college of education. It is now shared with the Chiltern Open Air Museum, which houses an interesting collection of rural buildings moved here from their original sites. Before the half-way point there is an opportunity to break off and visit the museum, which is open April-October, Wednesday-Sunday and bank holidays, 2 pm-6 pm.

The Walk

From The Stag go left along Heronsgate Road and left into Bullsland Lane from the T-junction. When this 'lane' describes an S-bend beyond the houses, branch right into a footpath. Go left with the path after 15 yards alongside an orchard (and its wire fence) and follow the path through to a lane at the far end – and turn left. This is Old Shire Lane at a point where it becomes a wide track. Now it's absolutely straight on for ½ mile along this very pleasant route, ignoring paths leaving from the right and staying with the track all the way to the valley bottom.

Your map may show a path going straight on from the valley bottom and crossing Newland Park. With the advent of the Chiltern Open Air Museum the path was diverted to a more circuitous route – the one which we now follow. For this, cross the stile on the right (the track itself turns left) and follow the low wooden fence on your left (about 280°). Ignore a branch leaving from the right after 100 yards or so and follow the wooden fence as it curves left and uphill under the trees. This fence soon disappears off to the left but a wire fence on the right remains (250°). This takes you up to a stile in a field corner.

Going forward along the field edge (180°), you will sample a little of what the open air museum has to offer in a distant view of some of its replanted buildings. The hedge gives way to a wood-edge which in turn veers right towards the lodge cottage. You should break away from the wood-edge and aim for a stile to the left of the cottage. At this point you could also break away from the walk and spend an hour or two at the open air museum.

To continue on the walk go along the drive to the lodge cottage. Cross the road to a bridleway opposite and follow this straight on to another road opposite Ashwell Farm. Turn left in the road and left again into a footpath after 30 yards. This runs between trees and a field

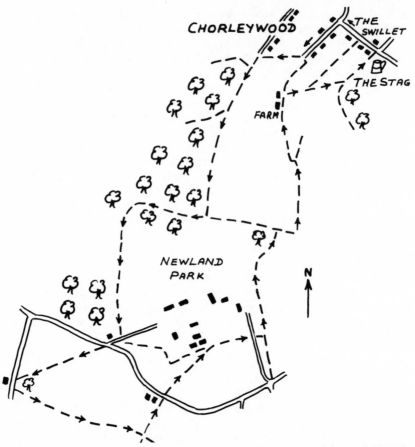

and shortly leads to a double stile. From the stile go forward (110°) along two successive field-edges (with hedges on the right) to a stile in the far right-hand corner, then along a short, narrow path backing onto the grounds of Rowen Farm Nurseries.

At the crossing ahead (there's a four-way fingerpost here), turn left to pass the nursery greenhouses and go along to the road. Cross the road to a path and stile opposite and from the stile strike across a large field, aiming for the furthest extremity of the Newland Park College accommodation block (50°). From a stile near the field corner you should cross a recreation ground, passing to the right of a very superior hockey pitch (floodlights and all).

Look for a pair of step-stiles that will take you across a college drive and over a wedge-shaped field to a stile. From the stile turn left into a bridleway and follow this all the way down to the bottom of a valley. Don't go left with it there, but turn right beside an iron gate, between fields and still in the valley bottom. After 90 yards go left and uphill between a field and an orchard. Stay with this track for ½ mile until you are alongside Bullsland Farm.

If you are not feeling at all adventurous you could stay with the track to its meeting with Bullsland Lane (you will remember it when you see it) and then soon turn right for The Stag. But for a little variety, and to help keep a footpath open, you could cross the field on the right, starting from the iron gate almost opposite the farmhouse of Bullsland Farm (ie the residential part). The route goes in and out of a dip (90°) and links up with another path at a stile on the far side. If in doubt aim for the furthest (upper) corner of the field on the hilltop opposite. After crossing that stile and walking alongside the allotments, you will find yourself back at The Stag.

Butler's Cross
The Russell Arms

Being situated on the historic Upper Icknield Way, it is not difficult to imagine the Russell Arms as a popular halting-place in times past. The present licensees are clearly determined to keep it that way by maintaining a high standard in food and comfort.

The bar menu includes 'starters and light meals' (soup, pate, prawns, mushrooms in garlic butter) and 'main courses' (steaks, fish, chicken), backed up by 'dishes of the day' from the blackboard. Ploughman's and sandwiches come under the 'lunchtime only' heading. The complete menu is offered every lunchtime and evening (12 noon-1.45 pm, 7 pm-9.30 pm) except Wednesday and Sunday evening. An extensive a-la-carte menu is available on Friday and Saturday evenings, and a roast lunch on Sunday. Children may accompany you in the dining room if having meals; but you will want them to be on their best behaviour in this elegant and beautifully furnished room! If the weather is dry and warm they would enjoy being in the pleasant, secure garden.

Real ale is ABC Best Bitter and Beechwood Bitter – the latter brewed locally. If you like very strong draught cider, try the Old Rosie. If you dare not risk the effects, try instead the Old English!

Dogs may be taken into the public bar.

Telephone: Wendover (0296) 622618.

How to get there: The pub is 1½ miles west of Wendover on the B4010. Bus route 323/4/5 from High Wycombe to Aylesbury via Princes Risborough (each has a rail link) calls at Butler's Cross half-hourly or better Monday-Saturday am and pm, hourly evenings, two hourly Sundays.

Parking: In the pub's own car park; but see the start of the walk.

Length of the walk: 5 miles (4½ if you drive the first and last ¼ mile). OS Map Landranger series 165 Aylesbury and Leighton Buzzard (GR 843071). Chiltern Society Footpath Map No. 3.

A lengthy walk but one of the least demanding routes to the summit of Coombe Hill. Approaching the hill little by little, you will enjoy the varied beauty of its green slopes, and when you finally reach the summit you will command one of the finest views in the Chilterns.

The Walk

I strongly recommend that you drive the first ¼ mile of this walk along the busy B4010 road as far as the entrance to Ellesborough Golf Club, and park your car off the road at that point. There is limited space along a part of this ¼ mile for both pedestrians *and* traffic, so it is safer to drive!

Starting from the beginning, turn left out of the pub car park and left into the B4010. Go along this to a bridleway on the right – almost opposite the golf clubhouse. Go through a gate by the National Trust sign and into a level bridleway. You now have one of the best ½ miles in the Chilterns, and with the magnificent slopes of Coombe Hill to hold your attention, the manicured lawns of the golf course (on your right) are hardly noticed.

At the end of that ½ mile you should go over a crossing-path, by another National Trust sign. Beyond this a gate will send you on your way for ¼ mile to a road. Go forward in the road and very soon left at a road junction (opposite an entrance to Chequers). Leave the road after only 40 yards for the woods on the right, where a footpath and two bridleways are signposted. You will need to take the footpath – the leftmost (110°) which climbs gradually up through the woodland. Ignore a branch on the left (with a white arrow) as you go, and stop at a waymark post after ⅓ mile (measured from the previous road).

The post is laden with waymarks – South Bucks Way, a Ridgeway acorn, and a yellow arrow. You should turn very sharply left here (almost in reverse) into the Ridgeway/South Bucks Way (10°) and continue gradually uphill through the wood, following the acorn

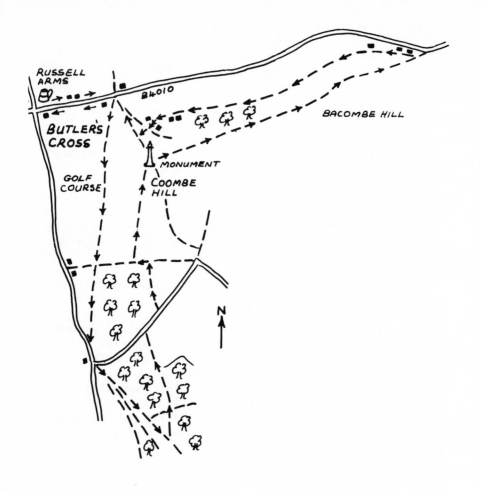

waymarks. There is a stile to cross (still inside the wood) as you come in sight of a field on the right, and before you arrive at a short drive. Turn left in the drive then right in the road and go uphill for 85 yards to a path on the left – once again in a wood. The acorns are still your guide and will remain so for another 1½ miles.

Cross a stile at the end of this piece of woodland. Turn left, then right after 20 yards to resume your previous direction. The open slopes and scrubland of Coombe Hill are below you and you will be on a slightly uphill route all the way to the Boer War Monument. A few moments relaxation at the monument will give you an opportunity to identify the Prime Minister's country residence (220°); also

Ellesborough church (280°) where numerous PMs have in their day attended worship.

On your feet again, turn right at the monument (relative to your previous direction) and take the slightly downhill route (80°), not the upper, level path. Alternating between path and grassy slope, you will be led downhill towards Ellesborough Road, Wendover. If doubt creeps over you while descending the third grassy slope, keep left and all will be well. When you come within 50 yards of Ellesborough Road, don't go down into the road but turn sharp hairpin left along a level path under trees. This path follows gardens on the right, then fields, and skirts the lower slopes of Bacombe Hill.

After meeting a stile ¾ mile from Ellesborough Road, you should stay level along the upper border of a paddock, passing a stable on the left. Leave the paddock from its opposite left-hand corner, and continue forward in a drive (part grass, part gravel) with two houses on the left initially, followed by paddocks left and right. At the end of the drive you will be facing the entrance to Coombe House. Turn left here and go uphill for about 20 yards, then join a waymarked path (200°) that runs up along the edge of the garden of Coombe Court (hedge left).

You will soon cross a stile and be deposited into a sunken bridleway. Cross the bridleway and climb the opposite bank to another stile, by the ramp or the steps. From here a narrow path under trees (280°) will soon connect you with a wider downhill path. Go through a horse barrier near the bottom and down to Ellesborough Road. If you have taken my advice and parked your car just here, you are home and dry. If not, do take great care as you walk downhill to Butler's Cross.

Whiteleaf
The Red Lion

Even if you put off the walk for another day, an excursion to Whiteleaf and the Red Lion will be a pleasant experience in its own right. The pub shares a short stretch of the Upper Icknield Way with a number of delightful cottages; and you may decide that, after lunching at the pub, a walk through the village (from Peters Lane to the Holloway) is all that you could wish for the day. Inside, the pub is cosy and traditional, clean and bright. Come on a cold day and enjoy the blazing fire – along with 'Doggo', the pub's enormous labrador.

From the 'Main Courses' heading you could choose from around a dozen items, and for lighter fare, from basket meals, jacket potatoes, salads, sandwiches etc, with stir-fried vegetables and garlic bread as 'extras'. The food is first class and nicely presented; not surprising, since the chef was trained at Claridges! (His omelettes and his lasagne are particularly good, apparently.) You can buy a meal any day 12 noon-2.30 pm and 6 pm onwards, but if you arrive after 2.30 pm don't feel that all is lost – the Red Lion is very flexible!

Real ales are Morland Original Bitter, Brakspear Ordinary Bitter, and Hook Norton. Children may be taken into the restaurant if having meals.

Accommodation is available in four en-suite bedrooms. One of these is a bridal suite complete with four-poster bed; so why not combine your honeymoon with the walk on Whiteleaf Hill!

Telephone: Princes Risborough (08444) 4476.

How to get there: The pub is 1 mile north-east of Princes Risborough. Approach from the A4010 along Peters Lane and turn left into the Upper Icknield Way.

Parking: In the Red Lion's own car park. Roadside parking is possible, but limited.

Length of the walk: 3 miles. OS Map Landranger series 165 Aylesbury and Leighton Buzzard (GR 819042). Chiltern Society Footpath Map No. 3.

A walk mostly along beech woodland paths, with extensive views across the Risborough Gap, and with the flowers, butterflies and birds of Grangelands nature reserve. Add to this a cricket pitch, a golf course, and a very steep climb to the summit of Whiteleaf Hill, and you have one of the most varied and interesting walks in the Chilterns.

The Walk

Go right in the road from the Red Lion and, after passing Holloway (a road on the left), continue forward about 60 yards to a signposted bridleway on the right. This is just prior to Thorns Close, and will take you between a thatched cottage called Up the Lane on the left and Pipers Loft on the right before dividing two ways. Take the left-hand branch (straight on) and continue uphill. At a junction of ways beside a Whiteleaf Reservoir notice and a metal gate, turn right (260°) and follow a fenced path for 80 yards (100 paces) to a crossing. Turn left here and climb the steep slope towards the summit of Whiteleaf Hill.

In a clearing near the top of the hill you will pass a grassy mound indented with a deep cross. The notion that this may be the site of a former windmill is not too far-fetched, considering its position. Further along, the very much larger Whiteleaf Cross is cut into the precipitous chalky hillside. This is also subject to speculation. One proposal is that it formed a waymark for travellers in prehistoric times.

With Whiteleaf Cross down on your right, continue forward under scattered trees along the summit. When you are half-way to a car park (170 yards from Whiteleaf Cross, and alongside a field corner on the left) turn left (120°) through a fence-gap along a path that soon runs inside a beechwood. Keep just inside the right-hand extremity of the

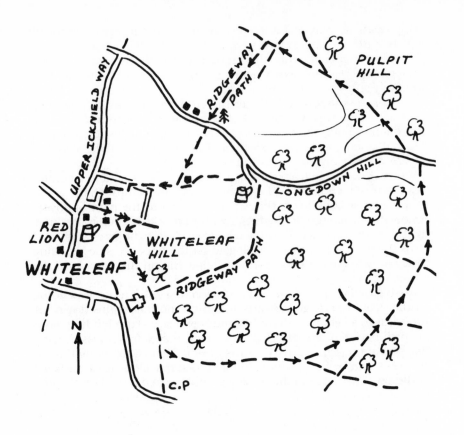

wood, and at a waymarked Y-junction after ⅓ mile branch left, obeying a white waymark arrow. This will take you through a horse barrier and gradually downhill in a good wide path.

After almost ¼ mile the path joins a bridleway that is also descending the hill. You should turn left into this and follow it down for 50 yards to an offset crossing. The objective is to continue forward from this point, but in order to do this you will need to go right a few yards and then left, resuming your former direction. It's now a straight run down for ½ mile to the road at Longdown Hill – with another crossing (and perhaps a little mud) to break the spell.

Cross the road to a bridleway opposite, and soon go through a nature reserve barrier gate, and follow the magnificent beechwood track until you reach a notice for 'horse riders' on the left. Climb the chalky bank half-left just after this and enter the open hillside. This is

Grangelands, a county nature reserve noted for its rich variety of flowers, birds and butterflies.

While you are enjoying the view, keep to the top edge of the reserve. Before the scrub restricts further progress rejoin the bridleway and stay in this (resuming your previous direction – 300°) as far as a crossing-path. Go over the crossing and turn left after 15 yards into a narrow waymarked path through the bushes. You are now on the 85 mile Ridgeway long-distance path which stretches from Ivinghoe in Bucks to near Avebury in Wiltshire. But don't be alarmed, we are walking only a very small piece of it!

When you emerge from the bushes strike across a field to a conifer wood at the far end (240°), then drop steeply down through the wood to the road at Longdown Hill. Cross the road to the path opposite. Follow this up alongside a hedge – with paddocks left and golf course right – until you reach a thatched cottage. Turn right here (280°) and cross the golf course to a kissing-gate on the opposite side. Looking back you will have a good view of Pulpit Hill on the far side of the valley.

Passing to the right of a cricket pavilion (the exact route depending on the state of play) go forward in a drive and follow this down for 100 yards to a yellow hydrant beyond New Place. Turn left here, into the path between houses. This turns right, then left at a kissing-gate. The path soon joins a drive (Thorns Close). Go forward along this for 40 yards and, when it turns right, cross the grass to a surfaced bridleway. Turn right in the bridleway and left in the road for the Red Lion.

Bledlow
The Lions

The great popularity of The Lions is due in part to its marvellous position – in a peaceful Chiltern village surrounded by some first class walking country. The guide books have it that The Lions was formed out of three shepherd's cottages. The licensee has other ideas – that it was purpose built in 1570 as a 'private way station' (a stopping-off point for private coaches). Whatever its origins The Lions is attractive outside and fascinating inside. Its low beams, tiled floors, old settles and open fireplaces (there are three) help to generate a traditional pub atmosphere.

The food is good too, with a wide choice from 'Hot Food', 'Cold Food', 'Salads' and 'French Bread Sandwiches'. On the Extras Board is today's home-made pie and a vegetarian dish of the day. As well as an extensive choice of sweets there is good real ale to round off the occasion, including Wadworth 6X, Courage Directors, Webster's and two 'guests'. The draught cider is good too – Woodpecker Dry. Food is available every day 12 noon-2 pm and 7 pm-9.30 pm, with the exception of Sunday evening. A roast lunch is served most Sundays. Normal drinking hours are kept, except for some flexibility on Saturdays.

Although The Lions has a family room, you may prefer to take the children into the cottage-style garden. And before you bring Fido with you, you will need to clear it with the pub's resident hound! Telephone: Princes Risborough (08444) 3345.

How to get there: The Lions is at the western end of Bledlow village 2 miles from Princes Risborough. It can be approached along West Lane from the B4009 Lower Icknield Way.

Parking: In the large car park behind the pub.

Length of the walk: 3¾ miles (3¼ miles if taking the short cut). OS Map Landranger series 165 Aylesbury and Leighton Buzzard (GR 776020). Chiltern Society Footpath Map No. 14.

A magnificent walk that you will want to repeat again and again – but with a price to pay in terms of stamina! A moderate ascent of Wainhill is followed by an easy ½ mile of one of the best bits of the Ridgeway Path. Then comes the challenge (unless you opt for the shortcut) as you climb a steep path to the summit of Chinnor Hill. Returning to Bledlow is easy, and ends with a mile-and-a-bit of level paths parallel to the former Princes Risborough to Watlington Railway.

The Walk

Join the bridleway just beyond The Lions and follow this uphill past the car park. The Swan's Way waymark refers to a 65 mile horse-riding trail from Salcey Forest in Northants to the Thames at Goring. Ignore a branch on the right quite soon and keep straight on up. At the end of the track after ½ mile turn right into the Upper Icknield Way – below a beechwood. This wide track is also part of the Ridgeway long distance path, and follows the contours of Wainhill for about ½ mile to a large un-named cottage at a junction of five ways. The view from below the cottage includes the village of Bledlow nestling among the trees and, further afield, the smooth promontory of Beacon Hill above Ellesborough. The town of Aylesbury is clearly identified – by one ugly tower block!

Go left around the cottage and into the uphill bridleway numbered CH38. (For the *short cut* stay in the level Ridgeway Path and continue for ⅔ mile to a right-angled crossing 75 yards, after Stepping Hill, a large house on the left; then skip the next two paragraphs.) Now it's steeply up to the top of Chinnor Hill – a real test of stamina! The path is soon in the form of a ditch and bank, the bank being the easiest and cleanest under foot. Ignore a branch going off left at the top of the hill – opposite an overgrown chalk pit – and continue forward, with any necessary deviations to avoid mud.

From the fence over to your right you can look down on Chinnor and its cement works, and out to the distance the Oxfordshire Downs. All around you is Chinnor Hill nature reserve, managed by BBONT – the Berkshire, Buckinghamshire and Oxfordshire Naturalists' Trust. If you chance to join one the Trust's guided walks around the reserve you will find it most interesting and enjoyable.

Having come fully out into the open the main path (now level) goes back under the trees, en route to a small car park. From the car park go along the road past two flint cottages to a path on the right, CH27 (that means Chinnor Footpath 27), opposite the entrance to Forresters Cottage. This fine path (not the branch going half-left at the start) is clearly waymarked by the Chiltern Society's white arrows, and will take you down to its crossing with the Upper Icknield Way/Ridgeway Path, having crossed a lesser path on the way. The Upper Icknield Way is unmistakable at this point, wide and chalky.

The *'short cutters'* should turn right here, out of the Ridgeway Path, while we all go downhill (soon between hedges) until the track curves left. At this point you should turn right to a level path crossing the fields, but if you delay this move for a few moments and go into that curve, you will have the inestimable delight of looking down at the rails of the former Princes Risborough to Watlington Railway. The Princes Risborough to Chinnor section of the line (this bit) was until

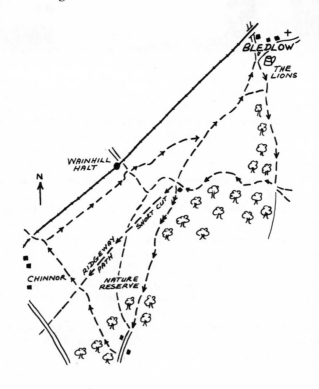

recent years used by the local cement works, but it is now in the
enthusiastic hands of a preservation society.

That level path across the fields is ½ mile long and runs parallel with
the railway. It then turns left and soon right, and meets a road at
Lower Wainhill. Railway enthusiasts may wish to turn left to see what
a fine job the preservation society has made of Wainhill Halt. Others
should turn right and left over a stile just beside a post box and
opposite a thatched cottage. Squeeze between a large shed and the
garden of Pixie's Nest and find yourself in a complicated arrangement
of animal pens.

Escape through the gates to the field on the right (aided by the
waymarks) and progress along the edge of the field to a cattle trough,
walking parallel to the hills. Cross a stile here and continue forward
to another (more a tall hurdle) at the far end. From here it's straight
on across the next field (80°) where the ploughman has (I trust) left
a clearing, then gradually downhill in a flinty track. When this curves
right keep straight on, but now across a field and on to The Lions of
Bledlow.

Before leaving Bledlow have a walk through the Lyde Garden beyond
the church. The river Lyde flows out of the hillside here through
an attractively landscaped garden, and it is freely open to the public.

Great Hampden
The Hampden Arms

A very ordinary-looking pub from the outside, but a revelation inside. When you are no further than the entrance porch the decision-making process begins, for in it there are three blackboards filled with delectable choices. In the two dining areas there are yet more blackboards, widening the choice still further. You could have a different meal for each of a hundred days, apparently!

There's virtually a full menu every day lunchtimes and evenings. And to wash it all down there are four real ales to choose from: Greene King IPA and Abbot Ale, Tetley Bitter and Ansells Mild.

Children are welcome, subject to the usual legal restrictions. Fido is also welcome, if he is well behaved (he might even get a biscuit!).

Telephone: High Wycombe (0494) 488255/488797.

How to get there: The pub is close to Hampden Common, a 3½ mile drive from Great Missenden. Take a left turn off the Great Missenden to Princes Risborough road after 2 miles and follow the road signs to Great Hampden – another 1¼ miles.

Parking: In the pub's own car park.

Length of the walk: 3 ¾ miles. OS Map Landranger series 165 Aylesbury and Leighton Buzzard (GR 846015). Chiltern Society Footpath Map No. 12.

An interesting ramble that includes Hampden House and some stretches of Grim's Dyke. Enjoyable for its fine beech trees and its mixed woodland, this is an easy walk with only one short hill − and a moderate one at that.

The Walk
Go left from the Hampden Arms and cross over to the unmarked lane at the road crossing. When the lane soon comes out of an 'S' bend join a path to the left of Martins Farm (No. 22). This path will lead you through a gate and along the left side of a barn, then between a wood left and a field right and eventually forward (30°) across a field. It seems that this slightly raised path hasn't seen the plough for many a day, which is very gratifying.

After crossing a drive go forward through a gap in the trees to a kissing-gate. Take the left branch of two waymarked paths from here and aim for Great Hampden church. There are three more gates to go through before you reach the church, which you may find locked, I regret to say.

As you walk through the churchyard you will see Hampden House directly ahead. Here lived John Hampden, recorded in all the history books as the Puritan leader who, with others, refused to pay Ship Money, a dubious tax levied by King Charles I. The house has changed since then, and was recently described as 'a very early case of Gothick Revival'.

From the churchyard turn left into a drive and, passing what was once the stable block, go through a gate and head for open country, walking between some fine oak trees towards another gate. Beyond the gate ignore the path cutting across a field and take instead the track that follows the field's right-hand edge. This is effectively straight on, although it does not seem so from here. Ignore a gate on the right quite soon and continue forward for 30 yards to a horse barrier. This is great: horses left, pedestrians right!

The two routes run parallel, with the footpath enjoying the company of some magnificent beech trees and the linear embankment Grim's Dyke. The origin of this earthwork is unknown, but it is thought that it may have served either as a civil boundary or as a defensive rampart, and that it could well date back to the Iron Age.

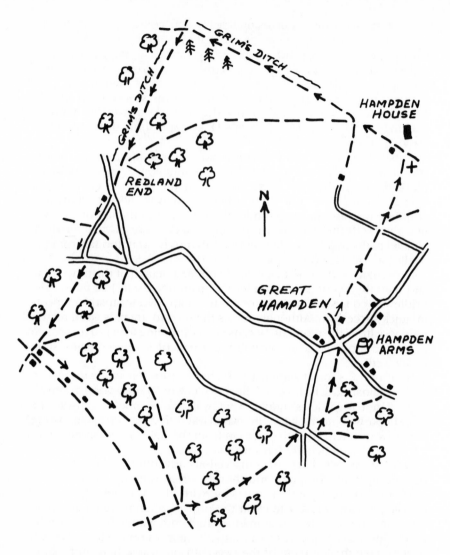

When you eventually meet a 'No Footpath . . . Hampden Estate' notice ahead, turn left and cross the bridleway to another path, resuming your previous direction but on the opposite side. You will then be walking just inside a larch plantation, as far as a waymarked crossing. There is a magnificent sweet chestnut tree at the crossing.

Turn left here into a wide track through the conifers (210°) and keep straight on over a crossing-track when you come out into the open. This will place you along the right-hand edge of a large field, surrounded on three sides by tall trees. Leave the field from its far right-hand corner (notice more of Grim's Dyke over to your right), then go forward along a good path under trees. When this path evolves into a track and makes its exit from the wood, keep straight on along a waymarked path under the trees. You will find yourself walking on the 'rampart' of Grim's Dyke for a short distance before arriving at a road junction.

Cross over to the Lacey Green Road and, passing the large house Woodview, follow the road to another junction – while noticing more of Grim's handiwork as you go. At the junction cross to the bridleway opposite (not obviously a bridleway at first sight) and continue forward, but now under the trees and to the left of a power line cutting. If the bridleway is muddy you could resort to alternative parallel paths over to the left, but be sure not to stray too far from the bridleway or the power line.

In due course the bridleway passes under a branch of the power line and then (by veering right) under the main line itself. Just before the bridleway comes out into the open, there are two footpath signposts in quick succession. Although ours is the second, there is good reason to ignore it for the moment, because by continuing forward to a rough drive and looking back you will see a pair of lovely cottages in an idyllic setting.

Back at the second signpost you should turn left (with respect to your original direction) and follow what would be a good footpath were it not for horses' hoofs! After walking ⅔ mile just inside the wood you will meet a carefully waymarked five-way crossing, where a narrow iron-fenced path comes in from the right. Turn left here into a bridleway (not acutely left into a footpath).

Once again we have that marvellous invention – a bridleway divided up into 'footpath' and 'horses', each running parallel (90°). Take the footpath option and stay with this through the wood, crossing a wide forestry track in the process and emerging at a road junction after ½ mile. Go along the Hughenden and High Wycombe road opposite for 30 yards to a footpath signpost on the left. You will need to take the left-hand of the two paths indicated here and follow it uphill to Hampden Common. A right-hand branch in the path near the top should be ignored unless you have left your car lower down the common – near the Old Post Office.

Bryant's Bottom
The Gate

The Gate gives a warm welcome to ramblers (even in large numbers) and to families with children. You may also bring your own food, for eating in the garden. Dogs are welcome, inside and out – with the usual proviso (I would imagine) that they are well behaved. Families can use the separate restaurant, as well as a garden and play area. Customers without children can decide whether they feel more at home in the public bar, with its traditional atmosphere, or in the more comfortable lounge or restaurant.

There is no 'rest day' as far as meals are concerned, a full menu being available every day lunchtime and evening. Although there are a great many items to choose from, the licensee is particularly proud of his version of that most basic of pub meals – the ploughman's. If your family is with you, eating at The Gate will not, in total, cost you the earth: the meals are surprisingly cheap and there is a separate children's menu.

The Gate is open for drinking 'all day' Monday to Saturday (11 am to 11 pm). Sundays are 'normal'. Real ales are Bass, Wadworth 6X, and Greene King Abbot Ale.

Telephone: Hampden Row (0494) 488632.

How to get there: Bryant's Bottom is 4 miles north of High Wycombe. Follow the road signs from Hughenden Valley.

Parking: In the pub's own small car park or in the road opposite.

Length of the walk: 3¼ miles. OS Map Landranger series 165 Aylesbury and Leighton Buzzard (GR 857995). Chiltern Society Footpath Map No. 12.

Bryant's Bottom is in one of three valleys that span out from the upper reaches of Hughenden Valley. Since the time is spent in and out of two of these valleys, there are a few steep (but short) hills to climb. This is lovely pastoral countryside, with very little to disturb the peace and quiet, despite being only 4 miles from High Wycombe.

The Walk

A signposted footpath leaves the road from the left-hand side of The Gate, firstly as a grassy slope and then, after turning left briefly, as a steep diagonal path behind gardens. After passing to the right of an upgraded cottage it joins a level track at the top. Turn left into this track and stay with it through farm buildings to a road. After just a few yards along this road go over a stile on the left opposite a flint cottage. Cross the field here to a stile a third of the way along the opposite side (290°). Veering right and keeping to the top edge of the next field (as close as the brambles permit), walk the level route to a stile and gate at the far end, with a valley down on your left.

Continue in the same direction but in the next field and aiming for an isolated cottage (Denner Farm). Cross a stile and pass to the left of the cottage along its drive. When the drive turns right go over a stile on the left and walk downhill in a meadow, with woodland on the right. From a stile in the bottom right-hand corner follow a well-used path steeply downhill through the scrub to a road. Cross the road to a rough drive opposite and go uphill through the ground of Grasscroft (the stiles should give you confidence), passing to the right of a tall pylon and making for a stile in the hedge at the very top.

Continue straight on in a meadow (260°) towards a stile opposite a corner of a wood (College Plantation), some way to the right of a cottage (Spring Coppice Cottage). Turn left in the lane here and, soon after passing the cottage, look for a path entering the wood on the right. I say 'look' because if it's muddy you could stay in the lane and turn right at the bottom (it's not far).

If you have chosen the path, ignore a branch on the right very soon and simply follow the main route (220°) to the bottom (Coleheath Bottom). Turn left, then right in the road by Hulton Lodge scout hut,

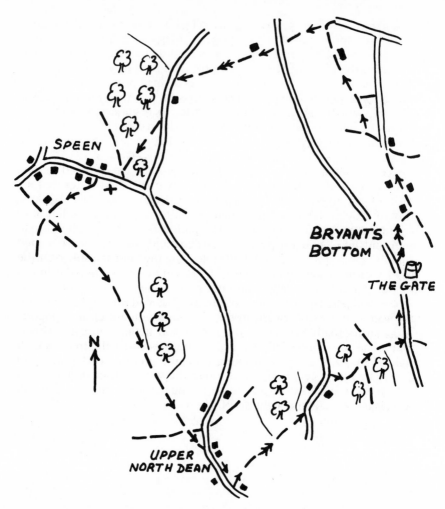

meeting up with those who avoided the woodland path. So now it's
uphill past Speen Baptist church and into a hairpin drive on the left
– just beyond the 30mph speed limit signs. Leave the drive after only
a few yards and take an uphill path bordering the attractive Pye
Cottage. You will soon be in a small meadow and crossing a stile in
its opposite right-hand corner. After that there are two well-fenced
fields, with stiles on the right to help you on your way to a crossing.
This is in the far right-hand corner, where a four-way signpost stands
close to a garden pond.

Turn left and follow a good fence (140°) along what is the highest level hereabouts. There is quite a long stretch now through magnificent open country, with fields on either side and a distant gap revealing the town of High Wycombe. The path (if you can detect it in the grass) curves slightly right, passes a small pond under trees on the left and aims for that gap. The spell is broken by a difficult rail on the left, which you must climb in order to resume your direction. From the rail you should draw closer to the wood on the left, while you make your way down to a farm crossing-track in the confluence of three valleys.

Keep forward over the crossing (there's a rail on each side), then over a stile and along the left side of a low cattle shed. After that it's a short step to the road by Upper North Dean village hall. Walking down through this delightful village look for a path on the left after a long house called Long Wood. The path is opposite an S-bend road sign and takes you up between gardens and into a field. It's then steeply uphill alongside a tall hedge, leaving the field at a stile near the top. A cattle trough marks the spot. Having crossed the stile into a wood go right immediately and continue uphill.

You will pass two old sheds on the right as you proceed straight on to meet a lane. Go forward in the lane until you are clear of Pigotts and join footpath No. 42 on the right opposite an iron gate. This is where the lane curves left. After only 20 yards under the trees branch right (130°) along a path backing onto the grounds of Pigotts, and eventually drop steeply down through the woods; then along a field edge to the road at Bryant's Bottom. Going left along the road you will soon have a welcome sighting of The Gate.

Great Missenden
The George

Dating back to 1480, The George is one of twelve inns that existed in the village in earlier days, when the High Street formed part of the coach road to London. Unpretentious outside and cosy inside, the inn serves inexpensive snacks including such unusual items as fritto misto vegetaire and (peppery hot) onion bjajis. The main menu and 'specials' from the blackboard include items ranging from simple pub fare to vegetable curry and fresh salmon. Meals and snacks are available lunchtimes and evenings every day.

The inn sells four real ales – Fuller's London Pride, Greene King IPA, ABC and Marston's Pedigree. It is open for drinking at normal pub hours, and has a small beer garden. Children are welcome, inside and out.

In the car park behind the inn can be seen the well-preserved Court House. This timber framed two-storied building is where twice-yearly sheriff courts were held.

Telephone: Great Missenden (02406) 2084.

How to get there: The inn is in the High Street and can be approached from the A413 road bypassing the village. It is a few minutes walk from Great Missenden station, which is on the London (Marylebone) to Aylesbury line. Trains run half-hourly or better Monday-Friday, hourly Saturday and Sunday. On Sunday the service is from Baker Street (change at Amersham). Bus 27/344-347 from High Wycombe bus station runs hourly or better Monday-Saturday only.

Parking: In The George car park or in the public car park situated near the other end of the High Street.

Length of the walk: 4¾ miles. OS Map Landranger series 165 Aylesbury and Leighton Buzzard (GR 895011). Chiltern Society Footpath Map No. 8.

After a moderate climb out of the Misbourne valley the path crosses a level but varied landscape of fields and small woodlands – undramatic but full of the simple delights of Buckinghamshire's countryside. Since it follows the well-waymarked route of a county circular walk, the chances of your going astray are minimal.

The Walk
From The George cross over to Church Street and go along this to where it curves left (not into Abbey Walk, earlier). Passing a triangular green and the C of E school on the left, go through the A413 subway; then steeply uphill in a tarmac path and through another subway. From a T-junction at the top of the path turn left into a rough track. When this soon bears right for Hill House, keep straight on through a gap and alongside a flint wall. A stile will lead you forward along a level path between fences and into Stocking's Wood. In the wood the path curves slightly right (0°) and runs firstly level and then downhill to a stile at the bottom.

Go over that stile into a field on the right. With the wood on the left initially, climb the field to a stile in the direction roughly midway between two distant pylons (60°). Beyond that stile continue forward along the boundary between two fields and, with a wire fence on the right, head for another stile near the right-hand extremity of a beechwood. Passing diagonally through the wood (half-left, 10°) you may notice the shallow earthworks which are the remains of a medieval manor.

Once out of the wood cross a field straight on to a stile and gate just to the right of a paddock – which has a large white house attached. Cross the road here to a stile and take stock of another wood, Hickman's Coppice, at the far end of a large field. Aim for a stile at the near corner of this wood (80°). When you get there continue in the same direction through the wood, reaching the light of day at the wood's furthest corner. From the double stile here go forward for 60 yards to another double stile, passing a wooden electricity pole on your right.

Turn right at this second double stile and strike across a large field (cutting off a sizeable corner) to a stile near its far left-hand corner. Since you will not see the stile initially, you will find a compass most useful by following a bearing of 110°. Pass through to the adjacent field and continue roughly in the same direction to a stile near the right-hand side of a house. From here go half-right across small fields to the road opposite Marriotts Avenue, South Heath. Join the path to the left of Marriotts Avenue, behind Willow Lodge, and walk the long straight path backing onto gardens.

At the end of the gardens turn right into a wide woodland path. This woodland is Redding Wick and contains the earthworks of a 12th century settlement, part of which you may discern soon after making that right turn. As you leave the wood continue straight on until you meet a drive opposite Wick Cottage. Turn right in the drive

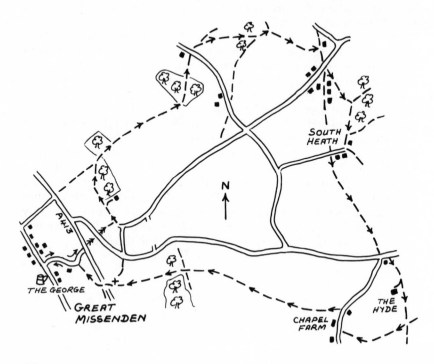

and proceed along this for 80 yards to a path on the left just after The Huddle – a timber bungalow. This path soon takes you into a field and along its left-hand edge. Keeping straight on you will then follow the right-hand edge of the next field, eventually to join a stile 40 yards left of the far right-hand corner. It's now a short step across the next, the third, field to a stile and the road at Hyde End.

If your limbs are beginning to tire or you are impatient to get back to The George, you could save all of ¼ mile by crossing over to Hyde Lane and going along this for ¼ mile to a path on the right opposite the bungalow Rowen Farm – just before the much more impressive Chapel Farm. I'll see you there after the next two paragraphs.

For the longer route turn left in the road and go along this for 50 yards and into the drive on the right by The Hyde lodge house. From the far end of the drive go very slightly left and then forward again along a narrow path to a stile, passing a pond on the left.

Now take care. Go straight on (180°) over two stiles and into a large field, but when the field dips turn right and follow the dip downhill, passing an overgrown pit on your left. Then continue in the same direction, but in a concrete farm drive and heading up towards farm buildings. When you reach the road up there turn right and pass Chapel Farm on your left.

This is where we meet up with the 'short cutters' and join a path opposite the bungalow Rowen Farm – on the left for us, on the right for them. This short path under trees leads to a stile and a field. Turn left from the stile and follow a straight ½ mile succession of level field edges. When the hedgeline ceases at a field corner you are let loose into what soon becomes a downward sloping field, which you should traverse half-left (280°). After crossing a metalled track continue straight on downhill (still 280°), but now in a sheep pasture, keeping slightly right of a dip and finally passing through a churchyard kissing-gate.

The church drive takes you over the A413, alongside the grounds of Missenden Abbey. The 'Abbey' is on the site of a 12th century monastic house. It is used by the County Council as a residential study centre offering a wide range of special-interest courses. The drive will take you back into Great Missenden and to The George.

Little Missenden
The Crown

The Crown is a delightful little pub in a quiet country lane not far from the village centre. In summer its cottage appearance is enhanced by colourful window boxes and hanging baskets. Inside, the small lounge area is beautifully maintained and welcoming, and its cleanliness exemplary. In winter you can enjoy the warmth of a real open fire, and in summer the large attractive garden.

Three real ales are served, Hook Norton Bitter, Morrells Varsity Bitter and Marston's Pedigree; also a good draught cider – Bulmers Original Dry Scrumpy. Bar snacks are available lunchtimes only, Monday to Friday – also on Saturday, but with a reduced choice. It is simple fare (quiche, pizza, salads, cottage pie, hotpot etc) but very appetising.

Children under 14 cannot be accommodated inside but they may be taken into the garden, where there is a covered area and enough to keep them occupied. If you wish, you may eat your own food out there – after you have bought drinks from the bar.

A free house for more than 20 years, The Crown has been run by the same family since 1920. On the walls of the lounge there is an interesting display of old horticultural implements, as well as photographs of the village in earlier days.

Telephone: Great Missenden (02406) 2571.

How to get there: The pub is ¼ mile east of the village centre and a short distance south of the A413 between Great Missenden and Old Amersham.

Parking: Along the roadside or in the small pub car park.

Length of the walk: 4 miles. OS Map Landranger series 165 Aylesbury and Leighton Buzzard (GR 926988). Chiltern Society Footpath Map No. 6.

A moderate climb up from The Crown gives some very attractive views of the Misbourne valley. After that it's mostly easy-going across pleasant open countryside. Towards the end of the walk the valley comes back into view, and there's an opportunity to enjoy the lovely village of Little Missenden and to visit its ancient church. Good footware is recommended for this walk, since part of it may be very muddy.

The Walk

Cross the road from the The Crown and join a rough drive to the left of the community centre. The drive passes Toby's Lane Farm and soon changes to an uphill path between hedges and trees. When it meets the corner of a wood higher up, don't go into the wood but follow its left-hand edge. The path soon runs between hedges and eventually curves right. Go over a stile (or through a gap) in the left-hand hedge here, and into a field. Continue in the same direction (160°) to a hedge gap, cutting off a large corner of the field. From this gap there should be a clear path diagonally across the next field in the direction of the left-most of a series of distant pylons (150°). This leads to a stile in the furthest corner of the field.

From the stile go along the left-hand edge of the next field, in the direction of two pylons and Mop End Farm (210°). On arrival at a stile and gate in the field's far left-hand corner, aim for the stile and footpath signpost in the furthest corner of the next field, just to the left of the farmhouse (the house adjacent to the barns). If you happen to meet the farmer, you will find him most welcoming and friendly; likewise his dogs – after their introductory barking!

From the farm go forward in the road for 70 yards and turn right over a stile beside an iron gate. Take the right-hand of two paths here, the one following a hedge and overhead wires. Go over a stile into another field ahead when the hedge turns briefly left, then veer right across this field (300°) to a stile on the opposite side. Cross a bridleway here (Toby's Lane) and proceed alongside a hedge to a lane at the far end. Go 30 yards left along the lane to a gap on the right, where a footpath sign directs you along the right-hand edge of a field.

You will pass Beamond End Farm (or Ranch!) and its gardens on the right, before dropping downhill accompanied by overhead wires. Lower down a gap in a field corner will lead you into a wood. Go down into the dell (300°) and up again (ie straight on) to join an uphill path lined with Scots pines, eventually arriving at a cul-de-sac in Holmer Green.

Go forward in the cul-de-sac and turn right at the T-junction into Winters Way, ignoring the footpath almost opposite. From the end of this road, at another T-junction, cross to the rough track on the right of Holmer Green Farm. After ½ mile (and after much mud, perhaps) this track follows the edge of a wood before entering it. When it

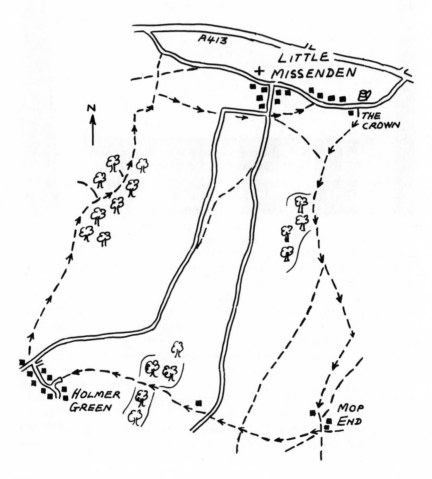

divides at a fork you should keep straight on (80°). You should also ignore later branches and keep straight on in the main path, eventually dropping downhill in a sunken path between hedges and fields.

Now take care. Soon after a pronounced S-bend in the path (and when you have come fully out in the open) you should turn right into a wide level path identified by a yellow waymark (ie not straight on). This path crosses a field and is part of the South Bucks Way, a 23 mile route from Denham to Coombe Hill near Wendover. At the end of this path turn left in a road and follow it (the road) round to the right. When the road turns left for Little Missenden you could go with it if you wish to see the lovely old church and the attractive cottages (turning right at the road-crossing for The Crown). Otherwise go straight on into a field along a clear path backing onto a garden (not the uphill diagonal path). This soon cuts off a corner of the field and leads to a road, which in turn leads to The Crown.

Penn Street
The Squirrel

A down-to-earth village pub where, if you come dressed for walking, you need not feel out of place – assuming you don't have muddy boots! The licensee expresses pride in his good quality beer: he sells four real ales – Benskins, Adnams and Tetley Bitters, and Burton Ale. Drinking hours are 'normal', except for occasional extended opening. Excellent bar food is served every lunchtime (12 noon-2 pm), with a reduced choice on Sunday; also Friday and Saturday evening (7 pm-9 pm). There is a family room, and a very large garden. Well-behaved dogs are welcome inside.

The Squirrel has served its time as alehouse, bakery and shop (simultaneously) and as a furniture factory. Today it is the headquarters of Penn Street Cricket Club, and from the garden you may see its members doing battle with their opponents on the village green.

Telephone: High Wycombe (0494) 711291.

How to get there: The pub is 2½ miles from Old Amersham, off the A404. Take the Penn Street turn-off. Bus 372 from High Wycombe, Amersham and Chesham (each has a railway station) runs hourly Monday-Saturday (early morning and evening only), two hourly Sunday all day.

Parking: In front of The Squirrel, or at the roadside.

Length of the walk: 3½ miles. OS Map Landranger series 165 Aylesbury and Leighton Buzzard (GR 923958). Chiltern Society Footpath Map No. 6.

An ideal walk for a hot, thirsty summer's day – with no less than five pubs dividing the route into three almost equal parts! And there's a mixture of field and woodland paths to give you alternate sun and shade, and very little in the way of hills.

The Walk
Turn left in the road from The Squirrel and left again at the road junction, then soon join a path running between a wine shop and a factory. Walking parallel to the factory premises you will be launched into a field from the second of two stiles. You should cross the field towards the wood ahead (100°), taking as your guide two incongruously sited manhole covers. When you reach the wood bear left and follow the wood-edge uphill (wood on the right, field on the left).

When the path levels out and the wood terminates you will be following the left side of a hedge under electricity wires. After a ⅓ mile of this long straight path you will arrive close to the A404 road. There is a farm building here, and a short piece of farm track linking the path to the road.

Cross the A404 to the road opposite, signposted to Woodrow, and go over a stile on the right after 60 yards. This is adjacent to Woodrow Farm Cottage drive. Strike across the fields aiming slightly left of the distant rust-coloured farm buildings (90° – not the farm cottage). When you are more than half-way there, go over a stile immediately to the right of a cattle shelter. Continue forward a few more yards and turn left to a stile and right in the farm drive. Passing the farm on your left follow the drive round to the right and downhill. When the drive turns right by the entrance to Tinkers Hill, go forward to a stile and very steeply down to the A404.

Cross the A404 and join a side road leading to the Queen's Arms, but before you reach the pub turn into the path alongside a cottage terrace. A stile will soon place you in a fenced uphill path leading to

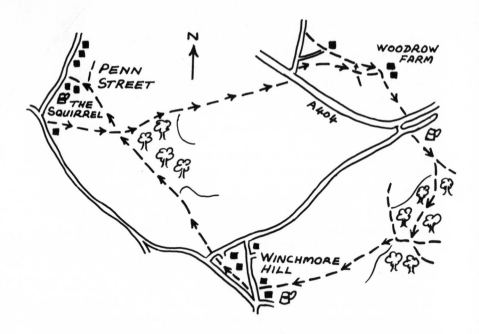

the nearest point of a wood. After only 20 yards in the wood, branch right (190°) under tall beech trees (with a field on the right initially) to a stile leading into a youngish plantation. Continue in the same direction through the plantation until you are back under tall beech trees – from a stile.

After 200 yards along a wide beechwood path you will come to a waymarked crossing-path, a point identified by a gap on the left leading into a field. Don't go that way but turn right (290°) into another wide path. Now take care. After 50 yards ignore the gap ahead, turn right and almost immediately left into a field. Follow the edge of this large field, with a hedge on the left, and similarly along the next field, accompanied by overhead wires. Join a path between hedges at the far end and emerge on the road opposite Winchmore Hill Methodist church.

Turn left into the road and go up to the village crossroad, where stands The Plough-cum-Windsor Restaurant, the actress Barbara Windsor's restaurant. Beyond the crossroad in Fagnall Lane is The Potters Arms, so if you are in need of a boost to help you along the final leg of the walk . . .

With The Plough on your left, turn right at the crossing and walk across the common parallel to the road, ignoring a footpath signpost near the crossing and passing the Memorial Hall. When the road veers slightly left near the cottage Orchard Rise, cross to the right-hand side of the common, heading for a bus shelter at the road lower down. Cross the road to a path on the left side of The Wee Cottage, soon passing between allotments on the left and a field on the right. This leads to a stile adjacent to the field's far left-hand corner, which in turn leads into another field. Cross this second field to a stile opposite (straight on – 340°) and follow a path just inside the left-hand border of a wood.

A stile at the far end of the wood will place you out in the open again, from where you have a choice of routes back to The Squirrel.

A glance around and you may sense that you have been here before – as indeed you have. The tip of Holy Trinity's spire (Penn Street) should be in view about half-right, and if you make your way across fields slightly left of it (330°) you should in due course arrive at a stile in a hedge beside a low-voltage pylon. Beyond the stile a path followed by a drive takes you back to the road at Penn Street. Turn left for The Squirrel.

Alternatively (after coming out of the wood), go down into the dip on the right, then turn left and follow the dip up to a stile (270°), passing a manhole cover and a cattle trough in the process. This is where you came in, a further stile leading you to the road at Penn Street. Turn right and right again for The Squirrel.

Bennett End
The Three Horseshoes

You would be hard put to find fault with the Three Horseshoes on any account. A beautiful inn, beautifully kept, with an unpretentious atmosphere and a courteous welcoming licensee and staff – husband, wife and family! In summer you will find the garden irresistible for the view it gives of the adjacent valley and surrounding hills. Your children will also like the garden, but if the weather is not at its best they can be accommodated in a dining area inside. And with the magnificent fireplace in the public bar, this would be an ideal venue on which to centre a winter walk.

There are nine items on the 'hot' lunchtime menu – familiar dishes like macaroni cheese, lasagne, cottage pie, gammon steak etc – and all reasonably priced. Alternatively you could opt for a ploughman's or sandwiches. The evening menu is more extensive (and a little more expensive) with twelve items, elevating to sirloin and rump steaks. The inn is closed completely on Mondays and no meals are served on Sunday evenings. Real ale is Brakspear Ordinary and Flowers Original (Whitbread).

Kate, the inn's resident labrador, is friendly to humans and, like the licensee, doesn't object to visiting dogs – if they are on their best behaviour!

The pleasure of being at Bennett End can be extended by staying overnight at the Three Horseshoes. Bed and breakfast accommodation is available in the form of three en-suite double bedrooms. Telephone number for enquiries: High Wycombe (0494) 483273.

How to get there: Join Muds Bank (a lane!) from the A40 ½ mile east of Stokenchurch and ignore all branches until you meet Bennett End Road (a narrow lane). The inn is near the far end of this road.

Parking: The inn has a large car park; just as well, since roadside parking is out of the question.

Length of the walk: 3½ miles. OS Map Landranger series 165 Aylesbury and Leighton Buzzard (GR 783973). Chiltern Society Footpath Map No. 7.

You may be pleasantly surprised to see a magnificent unspoilt valley only 2 miles from the M40 and A40 at Stokenchurch. The walk is along part of this valley and is overlooked from the north-east by Bledlow Ridge. It includes a visit to flint-built Radnage church, and for much of its length remains in sight of the Three Horseshoes – a comforting thought!

The Walk
Go uphill from the Three Horseshoes and join a footpath on the left soon after Whitethorns. The path runs uphill between fields and, at the top, passes to the right of an equestrian sand pit (you may know how better to describe it!). Now don't go charging on but turn right from the sand pit, as directed by a footpath signpost, and follow a hedge on the left (70°) down towards a large bungalow beyond the field corner. Once in that corner go through a hole in the hedge and, keeping the bungalow and its drive on your right, go down to a stile at a road.

Turn left in the road and follow this down past Town End Farm, an attractive flint farmhouse; also Charity Cottages with their interesting curved braces. From the road junction at the bottom go forward in Church Lane to St Mary's church, Radnage. Spare a few moments in this fine flint-built church, for its wall writings, its ancient font and its beautiful roof timbers.

Continue the walk via the steps in the wall (and a stile) at the far end of the churchyard. Then cross a meadow (110°) to a stile in the hedge opposite. That's half-right from the churchyard wall. Then veer slightly right across a field (160°) towards the far end of a wire fence near the right-hand extremity of the hillside trees. You will find a

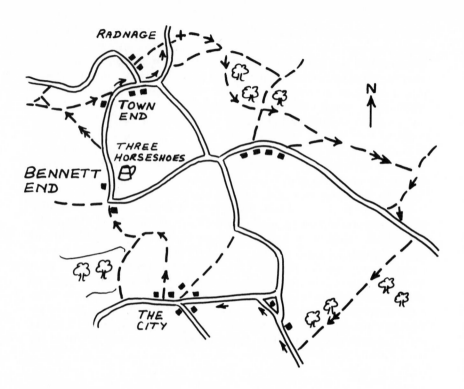

waymark arrow on a post there – which should instil confidence!

Following the upper edge of the next field as it curves left, you will soon be enjoying a breathtaking view ahead, with a hint of High Wycombe in the distance. You now have a succession of three upper field edges as you continue forward, with a crossing-path separating the first and second. In early summer you can enjoy a magnificent display of wild flowers along here, including poppies, thyme, scabious, purple deadnettle, knapweed, thistles, rosebay willowherb and great mullein.

In the third field your path joins forces with another coming up from the right (from houses down in the valley). Soon after this the field-edge describes a distinct left-hand curve, following a re-entrant in the hillside. After about 50 yards along this curve you should join a path that runs diagonally uphill between fences (110°). Hedges soon take over from the fences and the path gets very steep, finally making contact with a bridleway at the top.

Climb the very convenient metal steps here (or bypass them) and go right and downhill in the bridleway – but not before taking a backward look at the view. Pass another metal staircase on the way down (where the view includes the Three Horseshoes, at some distance) and join a road at the bottom. Turn left in the road and right after 60 yards into what is signposted as a bridleway, heading down into a dip then up towards the right-hand edge of a wood. Before reaching the wood you have West Wycombe's famous St Lawrence's church in view south-east along the valley, at a distance of more than 2 miles.

The 'bridleway' clips the extremity of the wood and soon passes along the left-hand edge of another. It ends at a road (Green End Road) where the signs disagree – one proclaiming a bridleway, the other a footpath. The presence of a stile *and* a gate doesn't settle the matter.

Turn right in the road and, when Bowers Road branches off to the right, keep straight on (in Green End Road) passing Three Pigeons – a lovely flint and brick house – on the right. At the junction ahead turn left into City Road and go straight on past Radnage C of E school to a footpath immediately beyond the war memorial. This path runs between hedges and then opens up to give a view across the valley to Bledlow Ridge. Beyond another of those convenient stepped metal stiles the path drops downhill, curves left under trees and is joined by a bridleway coming in from the left. After passing Woodways it meets the road at Bennett End. The Three Horseshoes is directly ahead on the opposite slope.

Northend
The White Hart

The impressive 'blackboard' menu at the White Hart includes a wide spectrum of choices from sandwiches and ploughman's to substantial main courses – with such popular dishes as beef, mushroom and Brakspear ale pie. A range of vegetarian meals is also available as well as 'Chef's daily specials'. No prepacked meals here: all food is freshly prepared on the premises and is available daily lunch time and evening except Sunday evening. Children are welcome in the Top Room and can be specially catered for. They would also enjoy the play area in the garden. Well behaved dogs are welcome where food is not being served.

Real ale is Brakspear Ordinary and Special and, occasionally, Old and Mild. Drinking hours are 'normal'.

Telephone: Henley-on-Thames (0491) 638353.

How to get there: The pub is a short distance from the Christmas Common to Turville road at Northend. Look for the large pond by the road junction, and turn off there.

Parking: There is limited parking at the pub itself, so check first if you wish to leave your car there while on the walk. Otherwise park beside the green nearby.

Length of the walk: 4½ miles. OS Map Landranger series 175 Reading and Windsor (GR 736924). Chiltern Society Footpath Map No. 9.

This walk is made up from two loops branching out from the Christmas Common to Turville road. The first gives a tantalising introduction to the awe-inspiring Wormsley valley, as well as some practice at climbing a very steep Chiltern hill. The second is largely a valley walk, half under trees and with just one moderate hill. The walk can be reduced to 2⅓ miles by foregoing this second 'loop' and returning to the White Hart along ⅓ mile of country road.

The Walk

From the White Hart go along the road to the right of the green, passing Chiltern Cottage and, on the left near the T-junction, a large pond. At the T-junction cross over to the rough track opposite (a bridleway) and follow this through a gate. Where the track soon turns left you have a preview of the Wormsley valley through a gap in the hedge, and another well after you have turned the corner, with Stokenchurch communication tower in pride of place.

Now you should not be so preoccupied with the track that you miss the waymark signs lower down the hill. This is where the track (now tarmac) turns left again, to disappear under the trees. The waymarks steer you off to the right here (70°) into what soon becomes a downhill sunken path under trees.

The next set of waymarks, on the trees lower down, indicate what is ahead rather than the here and now. The work of a retired highway engineer, I suspect! They refer to the crossing of an estate road at the bottom, where you should join S7, the track opposite (not a stile in the right-hand field corner).

Once again you should not become so absorbed – this time with the magnificence of the Wormsley valley – that you miss the next turning point. This is ¼ mile along the track and is easily identified: the track becomes a grassy path, there is a cattle trough (the second along this stretch) and a stile on the right, and the stile on the left is labelled 'Wormsley Estate'.

Climb that left-hand stile and make your way across a field at about right-angles (270°). Go over the estate road (again) and half-left across the next field (260°) to a stile and gate in the far corner. Go right into a track here and left into a path (SH4) under trees after 30 yards (270°). Take special note of a flint-built garden wall on the right because it is only 40 yards from where you lose sight of the wall that the path divides. SH4 is straight on, but you will need to go half-left into SH8, a cleared path (210° initially) between trees old and new.

The path is liberally waymarked and is never far from the field on the left, until it enters a more dense area of woodland higher up. This is where the stamina test begins, as you pull your way up the long steep slope. Take heart, for there is a delightfully secluded patch of grass at the top where you can rest and recover. This is on Northend Common between the dense woodland and the Christmas Common to Turville road, along a path that ends at the road.

If that hill has sapped the last ounce of your energy, you could cut short the walk and make a bee-line for the White Hart ⅓ mile away. Go left in the road for this, and right at the first junction.

For the complete walk (another 2½ miles) go right in the road and left into a bridleway opposite the first house and a deer hazard sign. The bridleway passes under trees and comes out opposite a one-time farm, where a footpath sign points left along a drive. Go left past the farm (barns converted to houses) and its garden and straight on in the shallow dip of the field (180°), ignoring a path leaving from the left and finally entering a wood at the far end, at a gate. After less than ¼ mile along the woodland track you should turn left at a crossing into PS24 (PS4 is straight on, PS18 right – for information only!)

This level route comes briefly out into the open when it crosses a farm track, and continues ahead along a shallow dip under the trees. After ⅓ mile it is joined by a farm track coming in from the left, before describing an impressive sweep around a pasture. The track heads south, with that pasture on the right, the woods on the left, and Rolls Farm directly ahead.

Leave the track when you are adjacent to the far end of the first barn and go left through the woods in a waymarked path at right-angles to the track. Stay with it as it turns left higher up and continue uphill along a hillside terrace (20°). When you reach an extensive storm damaged clearing (what a marvellous view it has left) keep more or less straight on until you find an iron kissing-gate near the top of the hill giving entry into a field. Cross the field diagonally and level (10°) to the far side, where there is a gate, a signpost, and a water trough. Turning left in the lane here, it's an easy amble back to the White Hart.

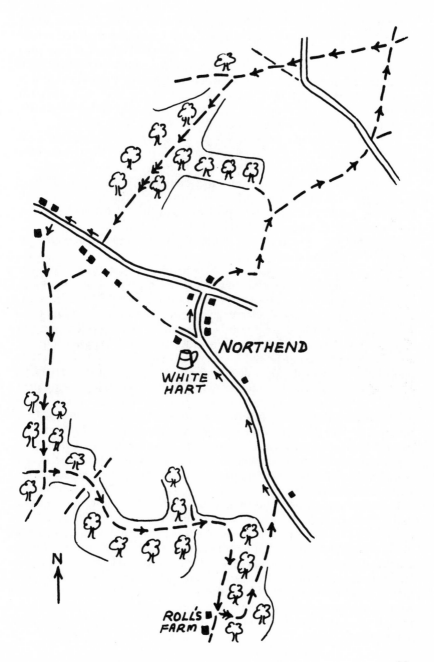

NORTHEND

WHITE
HART

N

ROLL'S
FARM

Turville
The Bull and Butcher

Situated in one of the most attractive of the Chiltern villages, this Brakspear pub traces its origins back several centuries. It is thought that the Bull and Butcher became an alehouse as early as 1617, and that the 'Bull' represents Anne Boleyn and the 'Butcher' Henry VIII!

A good variety of inexpensive meals are served, including some very satisfying hot vegetarian dishes. Chips are nowhere to be seen, which may or may not please you. There are usually up to 15 desserts listed on the board – and very delicious they sound. Real ales are Brakspear Pale, Special and Old. Normal pub hours are kept, with occasional whole day opening on Saturdays, and a full menu is offered lunchtime and evening every day, except winter Sunday evenings.

The licensees are happy for you to eat your own sandwiches in the garden when meals are not available – assuming you are buying drinks, of course. Children are welcome in the garden, but not in the pub itself. The same rule applies to dogs.

Telephone: Turville Heath (0491) 638283.

How to get there: Turville is about 8 miles west of High Wycombe, along the B482 and minor roads via Lane End; and it is 7 miles from junction 4 of the M40 – the High Wycombe turn-off. Take the Hambleden road from Lane End and turn right into the Fingest road after 1 mile.

Parking: In the pub's own car park, or in a small parish parking area between the pub and the church.

Length of the walk: 3½ miles. OS Map Landranger series 175 Reading and Windsor (GR 768911). Chiltern Society Footpath Map No. 11.

An outstanding walk around a trio of delightful villages – Turville, Skirmett and Fingest: each in its own valley, each surrounded by hills. We take one of these hills (all 550 ft of it) in our stride, we compromise with another, and avoid the steepest altogether.

The Walk

Cross the road from the Bull and Butcher and join a short drive opposite the parish car park. The drive runs between The Old School House and Turfelde and soon leads up to a stile directly ahead, and a gate on the right. I would take you over the stile and up to the windmill, but you might well complain of the steepness! In any case, the view of the windmill is almost as good here as it is from the top.

So it's a right turn through the gate and across a small lawn, then out again from the furthest corner. This will place you in a field and straight on in an uphill path (100°). You will be cutting off a large corner of the field and aiming for a stile to the left of a stand of trees. A level path will then take you along the left side of the trees and eventually to a road. Cross to the path opposite and stay with this (ignoring two left-hand branches) until you reach another road at Fingest.

Going forward in the road you will pass Fingest church with its unusual twin gabled tower. Sir William Connor, better known as 'Cassandra' of the Daily Mirror, lived in Fingest. He would have us 'look well at this ancient and sturdy citadel of Christianity, for there is none quite like it in all the land'.

A sturdy citadel of another kind, the Chequers pub, faces Chequers Lane. If you will go along this 'lane' for about 200 yards you will see the well-maintained iron railings of the village pound, where stray animals were once kept.

With the Chequers on your right, go along the Frieth road to a stile and gate on the right just beyond the last house and garden (there is only one). The path that starts here will take you alongside a hedge and up towards the corner of a wood. When you meet the wood keep it close to your right and follow its left-hand curve all the way to the top of the field. A considerable climb, but well worth it for the view; and there's a seat from which to enjoy it.

Go through a waymarked gate here into the wood, then out again from the far side and into a field. Cross this field by continuing in the same direction and cutting off a large corner (110°). This will take you back into the wood by an iron gate and along a wide path. Now be careful to turn right to a stile after only 50 yards (not the first path after the gate) and proceed downhill in a slightly terraced path.

When after 130 yards you arrive at a waymarked junction of paths, go over the crossing and straight on in the downhill path (180°). This curves right lower down, giving a brief view of a field on the left. After a long fairly level stretch it runs downhill in a slightly sunken path, then into the open between hedges and fields and down to within a few yards of a road.

Enter the bushes on the right just before the road and cross a stile into a field. Keep straight on across this field (250°) to a stile and gate (Skirmett is in view ahead) and along the right-hand edge of the next field in the direction of an aerial mast (280°). Over a stile and into a rough drive and you are in Skirmett, with its huddle of nice old cottages – and the King's Arms.

Turn right in the road and, after 100 yards, left into a drive opposite

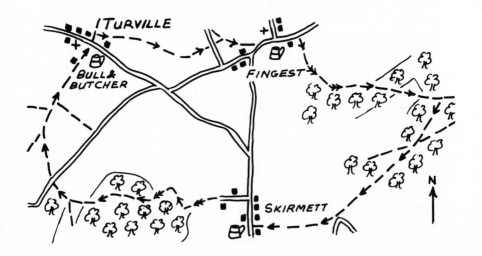

Fingest Church.

Meadowbrook. Don't be put off by the 'Private Drive' notice (it *is* a right-of-way) but go forward to a stile beyond what was doubtless once a farm. A narrow path takes over (there are barns on the right) and you are led uphill between fences and fields to a wood. The path turns right when it meets the wood, then left and uphill *into* the wood. Soon after it pulls away from the wood-edge (40 yards) branch right along a level waymarked path (280°). You are not likely to go straight on here by mistake, with that prominent notice 'Private – Vermin Control' to hold you back!

You will see the field downhill on the right and, after 250 yards, a 'Private Woodland' notice. Turn half-right (280°) here into a downhill path leading to a stile. From the stile go straight on across a field (290°), then under trees to a road, passing a gas plant on the left. Cross the road to a stile and go half-right across a very large field (360°). From the far side a hedged path leads into a cul-de-sac and the cul-de-sac into Turville.

Frieth
The Prince Albert

A beautifully kept pub in a rural position ¼ mile from the village. In summer it is difficult to decide whether to sit inside or out. Inside it has a cosy traditional atmosphere; outside there is a colourful display of flowers (no less than six window boxes) and a view across fields from the small garden.

A simple menu is on offer, lunchtimes only (12 noon-2 pm) Tuesday to Saturday. This usually includes two 'hot specials', a very satisfying ploughman's, and 'Jos's Plateful' – large granary (or white) rolls with a choice of ten fillings. If you mistakenly arrive here on Sunday or Monday, or if you prefer something more elaborate, you could delay eating until you are ½ mile into the walk – at the Yew Tree, Frieth. Alternatively you could be self-sufficient: the licensee is a comparative rarity among licensees – he is happy for you to eat your own food in the garden, assuming you are buying drinks.

All four Brakspear real ales are available; also Scrumpy Jack draught cider. And if you are just about to drive home, there is coffee.

Dogs are welcome inside the pub. Unfortunately children under 14 can only be accommodated in the garden.

Telephone: High Wycombe (0494) 881683.

How to get there: The pub is ¼ mile from Frieth village centre and can be approached from Lane End by taking the Hambleden road. Turn right from this into the Fingest road after 1 mile.

Parking: The pub has only limited parking, but there is ample roadside space nearby.

Length of the walk: 4 miles. OS Map Landranger series 175 Reading and Windsor (GR 798907). Chiltern Society Footpath Map No. 11.

This walk includes part of a lovely stretch of countryside shared with Fingest, Turville and Skirmett. It passes through the centre of Frieth, where there are beautiful flint and brick cottages to see, and also includes a visible link with the Turville walk in the magnificent view from Hanover Hill. Part of this walk is under the flight path of Wycombe Air Park, so if you are interested in small aircraft, this is the walk for you.

The Walk

From the Prince Albert turn left and left again and, passing a bus stop on the left, go along the road to a stile by a 'road narrows' and an 'S bend' sign – opposite the drive to a terrace of flint cottages. Cross the fields beside a line of hawthorn trees (250°) to a stile opposite Sunnydale, then go uphill in a narrow lane, with a good view looking back. Join a path on the left soon after passing a quaint flint cottage 130 yards from Sunnydale. This path runs between a hedge and a field, curves left and enters a long narrow field from a stile. A stile at the far end of this field leads you between gardens to the road by Frieth church.

For the Yew Tree pub and the general store, and some very attractive cottages, turn left; but to continue on the walk cross to the kissing-gate opposite. A narrow path takes you between a garden and the churchyard, then between fields to a T-junction. Go over both stiles here, turn left and follow a field-edge (80°). This field is L-shaped and you will soon be crossing its 'ankle' to the nearest of stiles at a wood-edge. Continue forward just inside the wood to the wood corner, where a five-way junction is waymarked – and where a stile on the left should be ignored. Now take great care to go half-left (20° and not quarter-left!) through the wood, after which simply follow the white arrows until you emerge at a road opposite Moor Gate Cottage.

Cross the road half-left to a rough drive and follow this round until you are adjacent to the house 'Moor Pen'. Then cross the grass slightly left (30°) until you find yourself amongst the trees and bushes along a waymarked path. The waymarks are very generous thereafter and

89

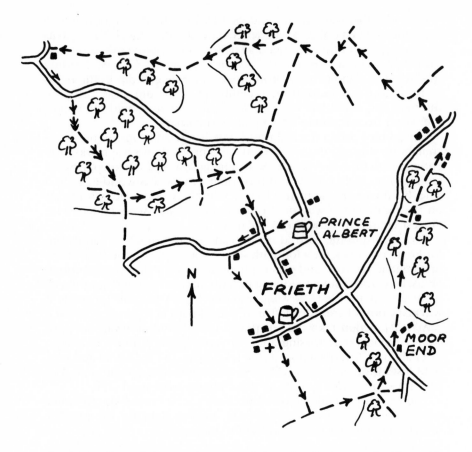

should instil confidence, the general direction being north. You will cross a stream early on (take the left-hand branch here) and, much later, the drive to April Cottage. The arrows continue to take you in a northerly direction and eventually out into the open beside a terrace of flint cottages (Diamond Cottages). With the cottages on your right keep forward to a road junction.

Turn left in the road and right after 60 yards along a rough track to The Verne. When the track soon turns left through a private gate, keep straight on under trees to a stile and a field. Now you should aim for, *but not cross*, a stile in the opposite right-hand corner. Turn left from that corner (280°) and follow a fence in the direction of a very impressive view. Cross a stile in the next right-hand corner and walk between fields and alongside a hedge and bank (330°), alive in summer.

Cross another stile at the end of this long field and turn left (a T-junction). Then follow a wire fence on your left (220°) for 150 yards to a stile, gate and water trough in a field corner. Go over that stile and turn right, with a wire fence on your right while you are heading towards woodland (310°). Drop down to a stile at a dip in the fields half-way to the woodland; then climb out of the dip, pass a stile on the right and curve left with the wood-edge. You should then enter the wood from the field's far right-hand corner.

The path crosses a track almost immediately and runs more or less straight on through the wood (280° and probably no waymarks) and enters a field from the far side. With a hedge on your left keep forward (260°) to the field corner and turn right to follow a wood-edge to a stile. It's now a simple matter to stay with the wood-edge (with fields on the right) all the way down to a road by Nine Acres Lodge, with Fingest church in view ahead (¾ mile).

Go forward in the road (downhill) and soon turn left at a junction, for Frieth etc. Look for a footpath signpost and gate on the right at the first bend in the road and go steeply uphill along a clear track through Mousells Wood (180°), following the waymark arrows and ignoring all branches. At the first crossing near the top of the hill (prominent waymark posts here) turn left into a level path (110°).

At a Y-junction take the left (level) branch and continue forward over a waymarked crossing after 30 yards (paths 5 and 6 crossing). After about 150 yards ignore a stile leading into a field ahead and bear right just inside the wood (150°), so that the field is on your left. The path runs into a drive, and the drive joins a road at a bend.

You now have a choice of routes back to the Prince Albert: either left into a field and down to a road, turning right for the pub; or straight on and first left – a pleasant alternative.

Hambleden
The Stag and Huntsman

A popular inn in a most attractive village 1 mile from the river Thames. Choose good weather if your children are with you, for then you can enjoy eating in the pleasant well-furnished garden, since children under 14 are not allowed inside the inn.

All meals are home-made from fresh produce. There is a wide range of interesting items to choose from, including French and Italian dishes. The choice is much reduced at lunchtime Saturday and Sunday, and no meals are served on Sunday evenings. Real ale includes Brakspear Ordinary and Special, Wadworth 6X and Farmer's Glory; also Old Luxters Barn Ale which is brewed locally in Hambleden itself.

Accommodation is available in the form of three 'character bedrooms'. For enquiries phone Henley-on-Thames (0491) 571227.

How to get there: The inn is in the centre of the village 1 mile from the A4155 between Henley and Marlow.

Parking: The inn does not have its own car park, but there is a good public car park nearby.

The water pump at Hambleden.

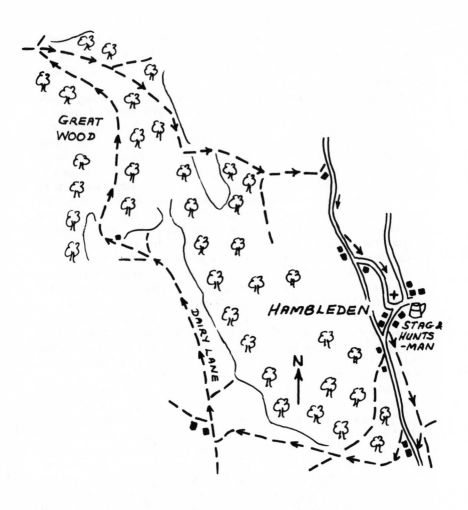

Length of the walk: 4 miles. OS Map Landranger series 175 Reading and Windsor (GR 785866). Chiltern Society Footpath Map No. 11.

A good walk for the enjoyment of Chiltern hills and woodland, without too much exertion or too much shade; there are views across the Thames valley and a magnificent but gentle ascent of Dairy Lane (a bridleway) taking the walker towards the aptly named Great Wood.

The Walk

Passing the church and the post office stores on the right, go through a gate on the left just beyond the tiny Hamble bridge, where the brook may well be dry. From here a path runs the length of a long meadow parallel to the road (about 160°).

Near another bridge at the far end of the meadow go through a gate and turn right into a track. This soon takes you up to the road opposite a house prominently dated '1907'. Turn right in the road and left after 75 yards into a bridleway beyond the last house (no. 41). This route is accompanied by a higher parallel path and follows the lower slope of Ridge Wood, giving a view of the Thames valley through gaps in the trees. Ignore the waymarked gate on the left leading into a field where another path crosses (this is the second of two gates), and continue ahead just inside the wood, at a slightly higher level. The path eventually leaves the wood and meets Dairy Lane, a rough track.

Turn right in Dairy Lane and, passing a pair of attractive 'AD1876' cottages, keep forward in this fine track along the valley. Ignore a 'No Horses' drive on the right quite soon and take the centre of three ways (HA37) after ½ mile or less. Ignore another branch (on the left) after passing a derelict shed and stay the course for a further ¾ mile.

At the end of that ¾ mile turn sharp (hairpin) right into footpath HA42 soon after you go under the first of some tall beech trees. This is the right-most of four branches in the path, two of which are rights-of-way as confirmed by waymark arrows. HA42 is an uphill track beautifully decorated by dog roses in the month of June.

Now take care: when you are a few yards from the top of the hill white waymark arrows beckon you off to the right. This is a half-right turn (150°) away from the present track (which is private from here on) and into a level path across a clearing. This path soon curves left, then right to join another track. There are fields well over to the left as you walk under trees for the next few hundred yards to a crossing. Here the arrows direct you left and soon into the open across the fields (70°).

When you meet woodland ahead it is natural to follow its outer left hand edge downhill, if only for the view. However, the correct route runs parallel just inside the wood and is joined 40 yards after leaving the fields. Whichever way you go, you will join a track at the bottom, which in turn leads straight on to a road. Turn right in the road and join a footpath on the left after a few hundred yards. This path cuts a long corner off a meadow (150°) and joins another road opposite Varnells. For the village centre you could either stay in the road or walk through the churchyard.

Medmenham
The Dog and Badger

The Dog and Badger has been welcoming passers-by for at least 400 years, a tradition well maintained by the present licensees. It is interesting to imagine the pub in earlier days, before motorised traffic shed its noise and dust against the timber framed walls. As if to make amends, the westward end of the pub (that end not facing the traffic) is in summer beautifully decorated with flowers. Inside, the pub is a delight: cosy, comfortable, and with much brass and pewter enhancing the traditional atmosphere.

The food is good too! There are separate bar and restaurant menus with an almost limitless choice of items, including vegetarian dishes. Try one of the 'extra large' jacket potatoes and this should set you up for the walk twice over. There is a full menu every day lunchtime and evening (12 noon-2.30 pm, 7 pm-10 pm). This is a Whitbread pub and has four real ales to its credit: Wethered Bitter, Flowers OB, Wadworth 6X and Brakspear Ordinary. Draught cider is Bulmers Original. Drinking times are 'normal' but extended to 'all day' during the busier summer months.

Children may accompany you in the Small Bar (there is no bar there!) or in the restaurant. The absence of ash trays in the restaurant is a silent message that this is one part of the pub where smoking is not entirely welcome. Dogs are 'no problem' in the Small Bar or on the terrace outside.

Telephone: Henley-on-Thames (0491) 571362.

How to get there: The pub is easily found on the A4155 midway between Marlow and Henley. Bus 325/328-330 from Reading to High Wycombe via Marlow (each has a railway station) calls at the Dog and Badger half-hourly Monday to Saturday (hourly evenings and hourly from Reading), two hourly Sunday.

Parking: In the pub's large car park or in Ferry Lane nearby.

Length of the walk: 4½ miles. OS Map Landranger series 175 Reading and Windsor (GR 805846). Chiltern Society Footpath Map No. 11.

This walk includes one of the 'least spoilt reaches of the river Thames – from Mill End to Medmenham. But before that there is one steep hill to climb (just one, I promise), a hill that presents some fine views both away from the Thames and towards it. At the midway point there is a chance to visit Hambleden Lock on the south bank of the Thames. This is accomplished by walking a footway along the weirs from Mill End, a very popular pastime.

The Walk

From the Dog and Badger go along the A4155 pavement opposite the pub's car park and, passing the 'WRC' entrance (Water Research Centre), go over a stile on the right in a woodland corner. This is about ¼ mile from the Dog and Badger and 50 yards before a road (on the left of the A4155) signposted to Westfield.

The stile is labelled 'CW' (Circular Walk) and will place you in a steep uphill path that runs alongside the trees before entering the wood itself. A magnificent view opens up at the top of the hill, after which the path turns left, apparently to a stile. *Apparently*, because that is not the way to go; the correct route being between wire fences, with fields on both sides (300°). Take care of the uneven surface along here.

Burrow Farm on the distant right makes an attractive picture as you walk between the fences to a stile at the far end by Chalkpit Wood. Once over the stile turn right and continue in the narrow path, now between the wood and the field. When you are adjacent to the far left-hand corner of the field, turn left under trees (340°) and walk 20 yards

97

to a junction of ways. Turn left from a waymark post into a wide, level path signed as 'Short Cut' (220°, *not* down to the road).

Immediately after passing a storm damage clearing (giving sight of the river Thames below) turn half-right (240°) through the wood, following the waymark arrows. This turning is 130 yards from the previous junction of paths.

A water treatment plant makes an appearance lower down on your right as you follow the meandering path to a stile and out into a field. Keep company with the right-hand edge of the field as it curves right to a stile and a narrow lane, by the treatment plant's entrance gate. Here is one of the best Chiltern views, including the river Thames and the hills above Hambleden.

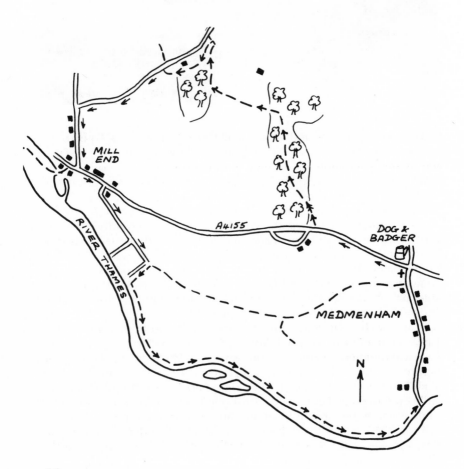

Turn left in the lane and follow it all the way down to a T-junction, crossing the Hamble Brook (which may well be dry) as you go. Turn left at the T-junction for Henley and Marlow, and go along to the A4155 at Mill End. A very short and most agreeable diversion from the walk is to turn right in the A4155 and cross to a footpath opposite. This leads to Hambleden mill, the weirs and the lock.

To continue on the walk, go along the A4155 in the Marlow direction, passing Mill End Farm and leaving the busy road shortly (and thankfully) for Ferry Lane, the first road on the right. Passing a house dated 1901, go left with the lane into a ¼ mile stretch, as straight as a die. Where the lane turns right at the far end, go over a stile and into the field ahead. Turn right immediately over another stile and soon join the bank of the river Thames.

You now have a delightful 1½ miles alongside the river to Ferry Lane, Medmenham. You will know that you have arrived when you pass a monument relating to the one-time Medmenham Ferry. But before you turn left into Ferry Lane, you will see the 'remains' of St Mary's Abbey directly ahead. The original abbey was founded in 1204 and is recorded as being 'very small, with no history whatever'! The ruins we now see are those of an 18th century building.

After the ½ mile of Ferry Lane, with all its fine residences, you come down to earth and renew acquaintance with the Dog and Badger!

Nettlebed
The Sun

The Sun being such a cosy, relaxing pub, it might be best to wine and dine there at the end of the walk rather than the beginning. The need to 'get up and go' would then be less pressing! In any case you might welcome more time to study the 250 or so jugs that decorate the ceiling of the bar. And with anything up to 17 tons of wood being burnt in the large open fire during the course of a long winter, you will find this a particularly welcome place on a chilly day.

Food is available every lunchtime and evening except Tuesday evening. It is all home prepared and includes chicken, fish and steak dishes, pizzas and burgers. Prices are very reasonable, and there is a list of daily 'specials'. Alternatively you could try the baguettes or the toasted sandwiches. Real ale at The Sun is Brakspear Bitter and Mild.

Since the bar overlooks both dining areas, it is not possible to accommodate families with children under 14, although they are welcome in the pleasant little garden at the rear of the pub. This restriction does not apply to well-behaved dogs!

Telephone: Nettlebed (0491) 641359.

How to get there: The pub is on the B481 Watlington road close to the A423 in the centre of Nettlebed. Bus 390 from London (Victoria) to Oxford stops at Nettlebed approximately two hourly every day.

Parking: The pub's car park can only be used during evenings and weekends; and since it is quite small, it would be better to park alongside the common while you are on the walk.

Length of the walk: 4¼ miles. OS Map Landranger series 175 Reading and Windsor (GR 701868). Chiltern Society Footpath Map No. 2.

The three-fold attraction of this walk is in the Warburg Nature Reserve, in the breathtaking expanse of countryside around Bix Bottom, and in the delightful common at Crocker End. There are two fairly steep hills to climb: one in the nature reserve and one at Bix Bottom. With these exceptions, the walk is plain sailing.

The Walk

With your back to the public shelter (not the bus shelter) and looking up to the Old Kiln (a well preserved brick kiln dating back to the 18th-century), go right in the road above the common. Follow this road past a number of attractive cottages, including The Malt House, and branch left at the road junction ahead. This narrow lane under trees becomes more rural after the intimation that it is the drive to Soundess House. In due course you will reach the lodge to the House; keep straight on here, in a track that soon runs along the inside edge of a wood.

Before descending a hill you will be able to read on a notice board what BBONT (Berks, Bucks and Oxon Naturalists' Trust) does and doesn't like to see in its Warburg Nature Reserve in the way of behaviour by the public. Perhaps you would prefer to know what *you* can see in this very special place – in the way of birds, butterflies and wild flowers!

While the track is still descending, and when it comes out into the open but briefly, another track comes in from the left, rear. There is also another BBONT notice board at this point. Branch left here (60°) into an uphill path under the trees. Now take care: after a fairly level phase the path goes into a sharp left-hand curve downhill, waymarked as SW31 and 'Nature Trail'. Leave the track at this point and join SW23 on the right (80°) by going straight on. This soon becomes a narrow path which in due course terminates at a stile. Turn right here into a track (the 'top' of Bix Bottom) and left over a stile after 35 yards. This is still SW23, part of the nature trail and leading into a lovely open area of grass and wild flowers. Sorry – picnics not allowed.

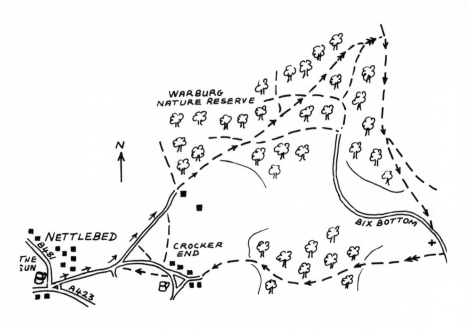

Cross the grass and enter the trees opposite (30°) along a path waymarked by a Chiltern Society white arrow. On a summer's day this path displays its treasure of purple spotted orchids, giving a marvellous sense of wellbeing as you walk through this fine place.

The path crosses another lovely clearing, goes back under the trees, and launches into a steep climb. While you are still climbing look for a waymark arrow on a tree by the corner of a wire fence and go right here to a T-junction. Then turn left (into SW23) and follow this steeply up to another T-junction, this time with a track. There are houses in view and a signpost proclaims The Oxfordshire Way. Turn right here into the track. A view across fields soon opens up on the left and the woods keep company on the right.

When after ½ mile the track goes into a distinct left curve, join a wide path on the right marked with a white arrow (180°). This point is about 100 yards beyond a gap (on the left) in which a Stonar Park 'Private' notice is displayed. The path becomes a good flinty track (between wire fences) before the whole magnificent world of Bix Bottom is revealed.

Go left in the road when you are down in the 'bottom', and join a path just beyond the ruin of St James's church. There is some evidence that this church served a village that has long since disappeared. It was abandoned in 1875 and replaced by another church 1 mile away in

Bix. The path (a wide track) is labelled 'Crocker End' and takes you uphill and into the woods at the top. Now you should keep absolutely straight on through the wood, eventually passing alongside an extensive yew plantation. The path is narrow here and soon places you in the open – at a stile leading into a sloping field. Soundess House comes into view again, half-right.

Stay at the top edge of the field when it curves left, and follow its hedge to the far left-hand corner. A stile leads you out onto a drive and this in turn to the green at Crocker End. As you walk the length of the green note the 'Nettlebed ½' footpath signpost where the second of two roads crosses. This directs you past the lovely cottage Merafield and along the left side of the green, finally to join the road by a crossing. If the grass is wet you could walk on the road instead of the green. Whatever your choice, if you continue straight on from the crossing you will soon be back at Nettlebed.

Middle Assendon
The Rainbow

A very attractive little pub, especially in the summer, with hanging baskets and a front garden set out with bright flowers. Inside it is conventionally divided into saloon and public bar, each with the appropriate furnishing – dining tables and chairs in the saloon bar, settles and scrubbed tables in the public bar (plus dartboard, of course).

The food menu is not extensive, but is perfectly adequate for most tastes and it's all home cooked, using fresh vegetables. The items are constantly changing, so that if you do this walk again (as I'm sure you will) you will find something different. Meals are served lunchtimes only, 12 noon-2 pm. While there is a full menu Monday to Saturday, on Sunday it's different, with a 'walk-in menu' to satisfy walkers and cyclists – soup, ploughman's, jumbo sausages and 'toasties' (toasted bacon sandwiches).

This is another Brakspear pub, and naturally offers Brakspear ales; these are the Ordinary and Special brews. There are no special arrangements for families with children under 14, although they are welcome in the garden.

Telephone: Henley-on-Thames (0491) 574879.

How to get there: The pub is on the B480 2½ miles north-west of Henley. From the Fairmile (A423) join the B480 where it is signposted 'The Assendons'.

Parking: In the pub car park or in the side road opposite. There is also an extensive lay-by alongside nearby houses.

Length of the walk: 4½ miles. OS Map Landranger series 175 Reading and Windsor (GR 738858). Chiltern Society Footpath Map No. 2.

This walk circulates around Fawley Bottom, one of three 'bottoms' that radiate from Henley's Fairmile (the others are Bix Bottom and what I like to call 'B480 Bottom'). It is 'the walk with views', for in this respect there are few Chiltern walks that can surpass it. The outward journey will demand all your stamina (there are two long, steep hills) but the return is a doddle.

The Walk

Cross the B480 to a side road opposite The Rainbow and turn left into the road signposted to Fawley. After only 35 yards in this road go right into a track beyond the last house. This is marked 'Oxfordshire Way' and climbs steeply uphill, giving marvellous views back-the-way. When the track comes to an abrupt end and gives way to a cultivated field, you should put inclination to the wind and walk uphill across the field (not around the edge!) while aiming for its summit (90°). There's a damaged stand of Scots pines up there and a gap in the trees to the left of a paddock.

Go through the gap and cross a level field towards the left-hand end of a line of trees (100°), cutting off a field corner in the process. There are two fields to cross, but when you are more than half way along the second you should turn slightly left and aim for the first wooden pylon that is clear of that line of trees. A stile in the hedge here will place you in a lane opposite Pond Cottage, where you should turn left. You will pass an ancient-looking farm on the left, before arriving at a road junction.

Continuing forward in the lane you may notice (after passing an incoming path on the right) the North Downs on the distant horizon – as well as a flock of llamas in a nearby field! When you arrive at Mavoli, the last of a line of houses, and at the drive to Seven Steep and Chears Orchard, it is time to leave the lane for a signposted footpath on the left.

The path runs half-left across a field (350°), passing a few yards to the right of an electricity pole (with wires branching three ways). It ends at a stile in the hedge at the far end, a short distance from the

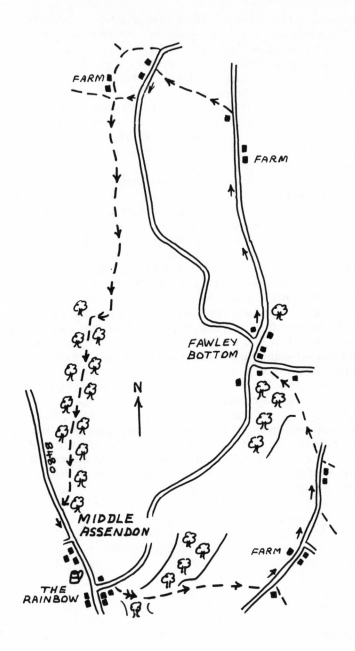

FARM

FARM

FAWLEY
BOTTOM

B480

MIDDLE
ASSENDON

N

FARM

THE
RAINBOW

field's far left-hand corner. From here you should cross the next field to a kissing-gate under trees on the left, half-way along the field's left-hand edge. Keeping forward and downhill from the gate (340°) you will pass a garden gate and fence on the right. After this a waymark directs you forward under beech trees and down to a stile and gate at a lane, where you should turn left.

At the bottom of the hill (Fawley Bottom) go right from the triangular green (Southend direction) and keep straight on in the 'no through road' from the junction ahead. You now have a long steady climb in this peaceful lane, with some incredible views into the bargain.

At the top of the hill you will pass a farm, a fine flint farmhouse and a pond, complete with ducks and dragonflies. Soon after the pond a flint cottage marks your departure from the lane. Immediately beyond the cottage garden a level footpath crosses a field towards the left-hand of two distant cottages (300°). From a stile at the end of this good path cross the next field half-right towards the *other* cottage. Once there turn left in a narrow lane and right after 130 yards in a concrete farm drive with two apparently conflicting signs: 'To Farmhouse Only' and 'Public Footpath'.

As you pass the farm buildings keep left in what becomes a rough track (not over the cattle grid) and stay with it as it curves left near the farmhouse. Now you have ¾ mile of this marvellous track, with fields on both sides and views that you will not easily forget. Enjoy every minute of it!

When the track comes to a sudden and surprising end, you will need to go half-right alongside a hedge (220° – the hedge on your right) and soon half-right again from a cattle trough. This will take you down to a stile and under trees, escorting you at first level, then gradually downhill through the trees. The path stays close to the field on the left while descending gradually. It eventually breaks out into the open and turns half-right (200°) heading downhill across a field to the B480. Turn left there for The Rainbow.

Rotherfield Greys
The Maltsters Arms

Attractively situated at a bend in the road close to the church, the Maltsters Arms is one of those irresistible pubs that simply draws you in. Once inside you will find that the bars/dining areas are immaculately furnished throughout. This is matched by the excellent quality of the food, which is not at all expensive and is served every lunchtime and evening. The menu card is conveniently divided into 'Pie Corner', 'Hot and Spicy', 'Hot Meals' and 'Quick and Easy'. On the blackboard there is a 'special' menu and a jacket potato menu; also ploughman's and omelettes. Vegetarian meals are available on request.

Well-behaved children are welcome for meals (with adults of course) in the dining area away from the bars and in the large garden, which has a lovely view across fields. Dogs are also welcome – on leads and under your close control.

This 'house' is first and foremost 'a pub with food' as opposed to a restaurant that happens to be a pub (a subtle difference), and being Brakspear's it sells Brakspear real ale: Ordinary, Special, Old and Mild.

Telephone: Rotherfield Greys (04917) 400.

How to get there: The pub is situated on an unclassified road 2½ miles from Henley. If you happen to approach via Greys Green, look for the war memorial and follow the road signposted to Greys church.

Parking: There is a good car park at the pub and roadside space near the church.

Length of the walk: 4½ miles. OS Map Landranger series 175 Reading and Windsor (GR 726824). Chiltern Society Footpath Map No. 2.

The central attraction of this walk is the National Trust's Greys Court, with its surrounding estate land. As well as the woods, fields and meadows there are places with exceptionally fine views. The walk is quite easy-going, with no more than two hills of any significance. For a perfect day out, walk in the morning, lunch at the Maltsters Arms and spend the afternoon at Greys Court. The house is open Monday, Wednesday and Friday, 2 pm-6 pm, April to September inclusive, the gardens daily 2 pm-6 pm except Thursday and Sunday.

The Walk

A short distance from the Maltsters Arms, and opposite the church, a footpath signpost has fingers pointing in two directions across fields. Take the 'Henley 2½' option alongside a garden fence on the right under tall lime trees. Follow the limes out across the field towards the right-hand corner of a wood (60°), and once there keep straight on, but downhill, in a sloping field with a marvellous view, including a glimpse of Greys Court. Cross a stile right down in the dip of the valley and walk along the bottom edge of a field (100°) for 80 yards to a stile in the hedge on the left. Climb the stile and turn left immediately, doubling back on your previous direction but on the opposite side of the hedge and still in the dip of the valley.

After a stile takes you into the next field, the hedge gives way to a wood-edge, and Greys Court comes back into view. You should ignore footpath no. 53 going off into the woods while you stay along the left edge of the fields. A private house comes into view on the left and a stile leads you under trees, and soon onto a quiet road near Green Place. Turn right here and go forward in a busier road. When this turns right after about 200 yards, join a narrow lane on the left and 35 yards after passing a drive (to Greys Court), turn right into a signposted footpath. This takes you under trees to a stile and onto that self-same drive.

As you walk the drive past Greys Court and its lawn towards the entrance booth, you might decide to break off for a while in order to visit the house.

From the entrance booth go left across the grass to a stile, as directed by waymark arrows (20°); then downhill alongside a ditch to another stile. This places you at the start of a grassy track, along which you should go for 100 yards only, to a gate on the left by a waymark post – a short distance beyond a footbridge. From the gate follow a clearly waymarked path under trees, soon turning right to follow a wire fence (10°), and then coming out into the open at a stile.

From here walk half-right across a meadow to a stile in a hedge (farm buildings in view over to the right and waymarks in abundance) and cross another meadow to a narrow lane leading to timber-clad houses. From the lane go half-left across the next meadow (350° and not necessarily in the direction of the waymark arrow) and enter the woods on the far side – where there is a National Trust 'Vermin Control' notice.

Ignoring a crossing almost immediately go forward through the wood following the waymarks and take care to stop at the next crossing, from where there's a field in view a little way ahead. That's 90 yards after entering the wood, or 110 man-size paces. The crossing is clearly waymarked and the paths numbered. Turning left out of footpath no. 30 into 31, you have ½ mile of level woodland track, marked by white arrows. When views begin to open up across fields to the south, path 15 leaving from the right should be ignored. The fields will be close at hand for much of the way, and earthworks (on the right) along part of it. When a younger woodland comes into view ahead, the path veers right and descends as a flinty track in the open.

At the bottom of the hill go over a crossing and climb a fairly steep path (280° and still no. 31) just inside the wood. From the top of the path go forward in a lane and join a narrow path immediately beyond Rocky Lane Orchards and opposite Rose Farm. You may be surprised to see 'real' orchards, but dismayed at the meanness of the path. This is shortly before the path turns, and descends to a dip. The ascent is mostly in the shade and terminates at a rough drive. Turn left here (or right for a short diversion to the attractive Shepherds Green) and, passing Lane End House, go over a stile on the right at the end of the drive.

Turn left from the stile as soon as you can (resuming your previous direction, but now in a field) and aim for the left-hand corner of a wood (100°). Go over a stile here and into a path running diagonally through the wood, but 'hold your horses' when you arrive at a crossing in the middle of the wood. By continuing straight on you can (perhaps) see cricket in play on Greys Green, as well as quite a lot of traffic (for the Maltsters Arms, branch right at the war memorial). By turning left you will have a little further to walk but a lot less traffic to contend with.

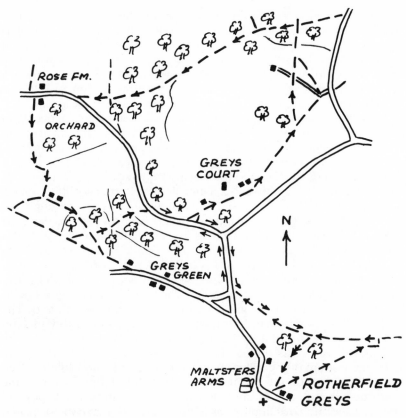

Assuming 'the lefts have it', turn left at the crossing (90°) and pursue this route through the main body of the wood and briefly alongside a fence to a stile; then downhill (still 90°) under more trees to another stile and out into a field. Keep straight on but now along the left edge of the field and down to a lane.

Turn right in the lane and right again in a busy road at the end. When this road turns right after 200 yards turn left into a side road and very soon join a path on the left under trees. If you have a good sense of direction and place you could now find your way back to the Maltsters Arms. If not, it's simply a matter of following the field-edge for ½ mile to a stile beyond woodland on the right. When over that stile double back along the valley for 80 yards before climbing an open hillside towards the Maltsters Arms. For a shorter (but steeper) return you could go over a stile leading into the wood just mentioned and follow path 53 uphill to a field, then cross this to Greys church.

Binfield Heath
The Bottle and Glass

Whether you are walking in summer or winter, you will find the food at the Bottle and Glass appropriate to the season. There are salad accompanied dishes in the summer – quiche, trout, eels(!) etc, and in the winter Beef Oxford, game etc, while across the seasons there is a wide choice of inexpensive meals which the licensee classifies as 'traditional country fare'. If you prefer something quick and simple there are various French bread 'sandwiches', which make a welcome change from sliced bread. Having started thus simply you should find space for profiteroles in chocolate sauce, meringue nests with apricots, or just plain cheesecake! Lunchtime and evening meals are available Monday to Saturday, but Sunday is cook's day off. For drinking you might choose from Brakspear Special, Old or Ordinary, or from the extensive wine list.

The atmosphere of this Brakspear pub is as appealing as its food – with its scrubbed tables, Windsor chairs, and large open fireplace. Unfortunately children under 14 cannot share in this pleasure, although they are welcome in the large garden. Dogs are permitted in the garden, but on leads only.

Telephone: Henley-on-Thames (0491) 575755.

How to get there: The pub lies ½ mile from the centre of Binfield Heath at the northern end of Harpsden Road. Binfield Heath is signposted from the A4155 at Shiplake.

Parking: In the pub car park or in Harpsden Road opposite, beyond the motor workshop.

Length of the walk: 4 miles. OS Map Landranger series 175 Reading and Windsor (GR 743794). Chiltern Society Footpath Map No. 4.

One of the easiest walks in the book, with virtually nothing in the way of hills. It passes through varied but unspoilt countryside where woods, fields, hedgerows, bridleways and footpaths are a source of delight to the walker.

The Walk

From the pub car park turn left into the Harpsden and Henley road and go along this for ¼ mile to the corner of a wood on the right. Here a bridleway sign directs you into the wood along a well-used track. Ignore the track leaving from the right of a small clearing after a few hundred yards and continue (60°) to another, larger, clearing (bearing in mind that clearings come and go as trees are felled and replaced). A grassy path takes you forward from here (40°) and soon out of the wood to meet a rough L-shaped drive. The base of the 'L' is the entrance to Highwood House on the right, and the upright is our direction – straight on. A track also comes in from the left here, its two branches forming a triangle with the drive. This sounds complicated, but will confirm that you are in the right place.

Ignore a stile on the left after a few yards and stay in the drive as it curves right beyond Upper Bolney House ('Farm' on the map) and soon left to resume its former direction. The 'Private Land' notices hereabouts omit to emphasise that this drive is a right-of-way, but the 'please' makes all the difference.

The drive is now concreted and very straight, with houses on the right initially. After ¼ mile a laurel hedge hides Southwood, then there is Little Spinneys before the drive curves left. On the right opposite Little Spinneys a path is introduced by a white arrow, and by an iron bar bridging a hedge-gap. The path crosses a field in the company (almost) of a string of wooden electricity pylons (220°) and ends at the right-hand corner of a tall conifer plantation.

A waymarked gap here places you along the right-hand edge of the plantation, with a field on the right. This wide path enters the plantation (in which you should ignore any branches – in the path, not the trees!), drops in and out of a dip and emerges into the open,

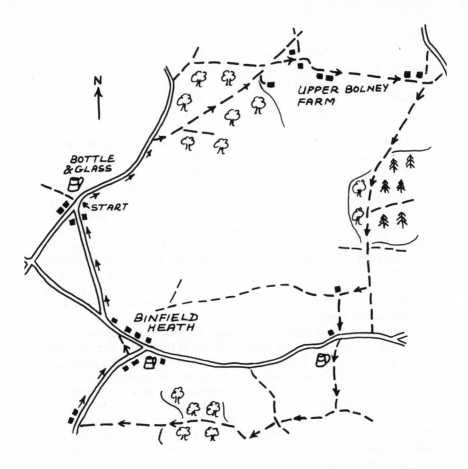

where a 'Hailey Wood – Private' notice requires interpretation. There is a gentle but pleasing landscape in view through a gap on the right here, and as you continue straight on between a hedge and a line of trees you can enjoy the company of field maple, sycamore, ash, chestnut and clematis – and a view across the Thames valley.

The path terminates at a dusty track, where you should turn right (the forward arm heads off to join a road) and go under our old friends the electricity wires. When you are alongside Kilnland, a part-timbered bungalow on the right, you should leave the track and go through a gap opposite the bungalow and along the right-hand edge of a field, following another string of pylons. This will take you to the road opposite The White Hart, worth visiting for its beautiful garden.

The next move is to find a path leaving from the left-hand extremity of the pub car park. The position of the metal signpost has been misleading and can, depending on the time of year, lead you into a sea of rape, while the correct entry is through a hedge-gap in the inner left-hand corner of the car park. From here a path runs southward across a field towards a two-legged wooden pylon and a small copse. You should turn right here, between fields and follow the wires, with the Thames valley well over to your left and Reading gas works directly ahead (at some distance, of course).

From the next (one-legged) pylon, and after about 70 yards, go half-right (west) across a field and over a crossing-path on the far side, then forward (290°) in a path on a grassy bank between fields. When the field-edge bulges out to the right the path continues straight on, cutting off the bulge. It goes down into a dip and, on the ascent, enters a wood from the field's far right-hand corner. In the wood the path turns right almost immediately, then twists and turns its way through to the far end, following a bank and ditch for most of the way. Once in the open this good path follows the wood-edge before running between fields (with a hedge on the left) and terminating at a road opposite Gable Cottage.

Turn right in this quiet road and stay with it for ¼ mile to a bend. You could continue to the crossing at Binfield Heath (for the New Inn, the village shops and a particularly attractive thatched cottage) and turn left there; or you could take a short cut across a park-cum-children's play area on the left. For the latter go behind a child barrier on the left near the bend and through a hedge-gap. Then strike across the park to its furthest corner and join the road there. Walk the road a few yards (rather more if you have come from the New Inn) and turn half-right into the Harpsden road. The Bottle and Glass is at the far end waiting to welcome you.

Hailey
The King William IV

With few 'traditional' pubs now left in the Chilterns (or so I am frequently told), it would be a serious omission not to start a walk from this prime example. Situated off the beaten track in a lovely position overlooking the Chiltern countryside, the King William IV (a listed building) dates back in part to the 16th century. It had a higher profile in earlier days, when the now quiet lane over which it looks was a minor coach road carrying traffic up from the Thames crossing at Moulsford. The fact that coaching horses were changed here is reflected in the licensee's special interest – he keeps a magnificent pedigree shire in a paddock close to the pub. He is also an enthusiastic collector of 'country bygones', and has these on display both inside and out.

Being a traditional pub you will be offered traditional pub food – ploughman's, hot pies, filled rolls and, in the winter, thick home-made soup (every lunchtime 12 noon-2 pm; rolls only in the evening). This simple fare can be enjoyed in the interesting but comfortable dining areas along with a glass of Brakspear real ale (Ordinary, Special, Old, and Mild) dispensed by gravity from floor-level casks. And a welcome rarity in these parts is the good old-fashioned 'scrumpy' – cask conditioned cider from Hereford.

Children are welcome in the main dining area if having food. Dogs are less privileged (the district council's ruling!) and must be tied up outside.

Telephone: Wallingford (0491) 680675.

How to get there: Hailey is 3 miles south-east of Wallingford and is signposted from the A4074 a short distance south of the A4074/A423 roundabout.

Parking: The King William IV has its own small car park. Limited roadside parking is possible.

Length of the walk: 3¾ miles. OS Map Landranger series 175 Reading and Windsor (GR 643858). Chiltern Society Footpath Map No. 15.

This can justly be described as a classic Chiltern walk, enjoying views of the escarpment at close hand, the Oxfordshire Downs along the horizon, and green fields and hedges on all sides. With only one moderately steep hill to climb (before the final run in to Hailey), this adds up to a very pleasant, undemanding walk.

The Walk

From the King William IV go right in the lane and follow this down to a T-junction, while enjoying a view of the Oxfordshire Downs. Turn left at the junction (you could have cut off a small corner of the field here and helped to keep one short footpath open), go over a road crossing quite soon (for Ipsden and Woodcote) and downhill to a T-junction by Ipsden village hall. There are two good houses along the road on the right – The Old Post House and The Old Vicarage. A pleasant short diversion, if you so wish.

Join the footpath immediately to the right of the village hall and follow this behind gardens and along the dip of a shallow valley. You have ½ mile of this straight path (with a hedge on the right all the way) before meeting a path coming up from the road.

Now you could be forgiven for taking the wrong route from this point by walking along the right-hand side of the next hedge, in the same general direction as previously; it's an easy and pleasant way to go. If you do make that mistake you could drop down to the road through a waymarked hole in the hedge about 80 yards before the hedge terminates and gives way to a wood. The correct route is a restricted passage between a wire fence and the left side of the hedge, firstly in an anticlockwise curve and then straight on again parallel to the dip of the valley. The restriction ends at a stile, after which you should follow the right-hand edge of a field to another stile leading on to the road.

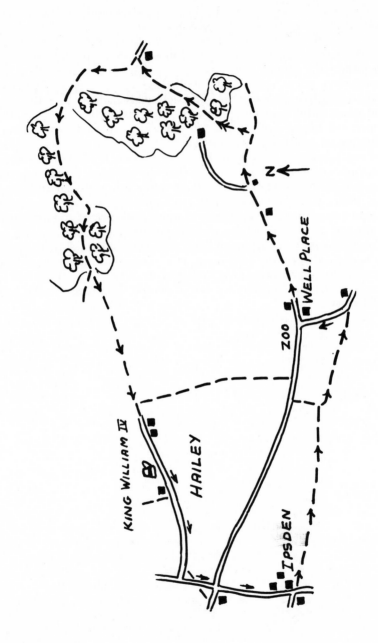

WELL PLACE

ZOO

KING WILLIAM IV

HAILEY

IPSDEN

Whichever route you are in, turn left in the road and right at the bottom into Urquhart Lane, by Well Place Zoo. The lane gradually degrades and passes Lower Handsmooth Farm (a bungalow) before meeting a concrete farm drive. As you cross this drive into the track opposite you should start counting. About 250 man-size or 300 woman-size paces (200 yards) will place you at a point where a waymarked branch leaves from the left. This path mounts the bank and heads uphill under trees. There are fields on both sides, and an impressive house over to the left (Handsmooth itself) can be seen enjoying an impressive view.

Cross a track at a slightly higher level than the house and climb the stile opposite leading into a wood. Note the waymark arrow directing you straight on through the wood (30°) to a stile at the far end. From this point strike across a field (50°) to a stile and gate on the left-hand side of a very nice house (Homer Cottage). This places you on a drive at the top of the hill, where you should turn left.

It's a straight run back from here, with very little to slow the pace. Soon after describing an S-bend as it passes through a woodland clearing, the drive (now a track) divides into two. Take the left-hand branch (260°) and make your way downhill, eventually to the King William IV.

Checkendon
The Four Horseshoes

You will likely come away from the Four Horseshoes with a few very firm impressions – the friendliness and politeness of the licensees and their staff, the way that the menus satisfy all tastes and all pockets, and the attractiveness of the pub and its garden. There are four menus: the bar menu, the main menu, the Sunday lunch menu (not just roast beef and Yorkshire pudding) and the barbecue menu. The barbecue is set up at weekends and is very popular with families. This, and the fact that there is a play area and that part of the garden is covered, makes this a suitable venue for children. They can also be accommodated in the restaurant area if having meals.

Meals are available every lunchtime and evening (12 noon-2.30 pm, 6.30 pm-9.30 pm) but with a reduced bar menu on Sunday evenings (7.30 pm-9 pm). If you are walking on Saturday you could call in for a drink any time between 11 am and 11 pm. On other days the opening times are 'normal'. And if you are into real ale you can choose from Brakspear Ordinary and Special. Dogs are welcome, but only in the garden and only if kept well at heel.

Telephone: Checkendon (0491) 680325.

How to get there: The pub is near Checkendon church ¾ mile from the A4074, midway between Reading and Wallingford.

Parking: In the pub car park or beside the church or village hall.

Length of the walk: 3½ miles. OS Map Landranger series 175 Reading and Windsor (GR 663828). Chiltern Society Footpath Maps 15 and 16.

The first phase of this walk is along level paths, tracks and lanes, sometimes shaded by trees, sometimes not. After that it is a complete contrast, with steep hills and hillside views in abundance. We climb one-and-a-bit of these hills before returning to Checkendon, where cottages and church together make a delightful conclusion to the walk.

The Walk

With the Four Horseshoes on your left, go along the 'main' road for 200 yards to a stile and metal gate on the left where the road bends right. Taking directions from the yellow waymark arrow, cross the field here towards its furthest corner. That's 200° or half-left if you are facing along the road. There's a stile to the right of that corner which will place you on a narrow bridleway crossing. Turn right into this and follow it under trees to a road – the one that you've just left.

Turn left in the road and, soon after passing Chestnuts, go right in the lane signposted to Hammonds Farm. When after ¼ mile the lane turns right to become a rough drive to the farm, continue forward in a track. When this turns left around a small beechwood, continue forward again, but now in a grassy path along the edge of Hammonds Wood. Ignore a branch on the right after 80 yards and continue forward over a crossing and deeper into the wood (270°). There is a Woodland Trust sign just before the crossing; this society is dedicated to the conservation and maintenance of broadleaved woodland.

During its descent somewhat later the path provides a magnificent view towards the Oxfordshire Downs (and the Didcot cooling towers) through a gap on the left. It then continues downhill between fields and trees, finally meeting a road at the bottom, with another magnificent view.

Turn right in the road and, when it curves right, go over a stile on the left alongside the drive to Bottom Farm House. Cross the field here to a stile in the far left-hand corner (10°). This is a diversion from an earlier route and may not be shown as such on your map. You will then be following a path that runs around the back of the garden (30°) and its tennis court, and along to a stile. From here cross the two

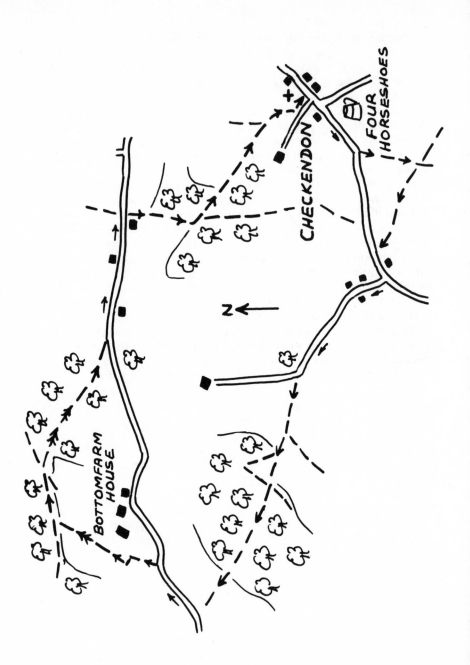

left-hand fields uphill (30°) to a stile in a fence below Heycroft Wood – a lovely place to stop for that flask of tea.

There is now a short, steep few yards under the trees assisted by hand rails before joining a descending path at a T-junction. Turn right in this path and follow it all the way down to a crossing-track in a clearing (a track opening out to a field on the right). Cross the track diagonally (90° – straight on) to a path that soon becomes a very steep uphill track. Ignoring all branches stay in the main route all the way to a road, the final part under the escort of overhead electricity wires.

Go forward in the road for ¼ mile, passing a cabinetmaker's workshop at the start and joining a path on the right immediately beyond the second pair of semi-detached cottages. The path is at right-angles to the road and crosses a stile before running just inside a wood. It turns left and enters the wood proper and then divides two ways beyond a pond. Take the left-hand branch (130° – straight on) and soon join an iron fence and a paddock on the left. This iron fence is your guide (except for a short timbered stretch) all the way to Checkendon church, where you can either walk left through the churchyard or along the Checkendon Court drive.

As you stand amongst the village's lovely old houses, the Four Horseshoes will be in sight, but before you make your way there, do go inside the church and see the beautifully restored nave roof.

Goring-on-Thames
The John Barleycorn

If you are a fraction over six feet tall the low beams which add to the attraction of this inn can be a hazard. Once seated, nothing but pleasure awaits you, especially if your appetite can encompass a spectrum of dishes that includes mussels in spiced wine sauce, moussaka, and sausage and mash. The licensee takes pride in his mushroom bistingo and Somerset fish pie. Desserts include raspberry pavlova, sherry trifle and (whatever next?) 'death by chocolate'.

Accompanied children can share in all this, in the main dining area or in the garden. And there's a full menu every day 12 noon-2 pm and 7 pm-10 pm, with a special lunch available on Sundays. Being a Brakspear inn, two of their real ales are on offer – Ordinary and Special. Drinking hours are 10 am-2.30 pm and 6 pm-11 pm Monday-Saturday; 12 noon-3 pm and 7 pm-10.30 pm Sunday.

Your dog is welcome, but in the public bar only, and on a lead. You can also eat in there, so he won't feel lonely! Bed and breakfast accommodation is available, the phone number for enquiries being Goring-on-Thames (0491) 872509.

How to get there: The inn is at the junction of Manor Road and Station Road. Trains from London (Paddington) to Didcot stop here half-hourly Monday-Saturday, one to two hourly Sunday (change at Reading). Bus 5 from Oxford to Reading calls at Streatley, hourly Monday-Saturday only. Streatley is over the Thames bridge from Goring.

Parking: Although it isn't possible to park at the John Barleycorn, there is a free public car park not far away off Station Road, and limited roadside parking in Manor Road.

Length of the walk: 4½ miles. OS Map Landranger series 175 Reading and Windsor (GR 598806). Chiltern Society Footpath Map No. 16.

This walk culminates in a delightful 1½ miles of Thames riverside path south of Goring. Before that there is a very gentle ascent 'inland' along cultivated fields and through the Great Chalk Wood, with an occasional view of the Thames valley and the hills beyond.

The Walk

From the John Barleycorn walk along Station Road and turn left immediately after the Catherine Wheel inn. This will take you past the car park and along to the High Street. Turn right into High Street and go up to the railway bridge. At a T-junction just beyond the bridge turn right, then left into the B4526 by the Queen's Arms. Whitehills Green is second on the right along the B4526 and you should follow this between new Georgian-style houses as it turns left and ends near a small triangular pavement. On the right there is a short path between hedges that ends at a stile. From here cross a recreation ground to a stile in the far left-hand corner (130°), not to be confused with another stile 50 yards to the right of this.

From that corner stile go uphill (80°) along the left edge of a sloping field, with a hedge on the left. At the summit of the path a stile leads into another field, and there's more of the same until the path turns right from the far left-hand corner. It's downhill now, to a stile in a corner just above a dip in the field, then to another stile after a few yards and uphill under trees.

The clear path runs up into the wood at about 110° for ⅓ mile (becoming wider in the process and marked by yellow arrows) before levelling out and meeting a forestry crossing-track. Now you must keep your wits about you and start counting! Cross the track and continue for 80 yards *only*, that's about 100 man-size paces, until you see an uphill path leaving from the right (260° – doubling back

125

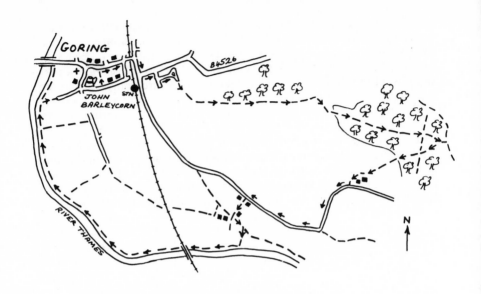

slightly). This is just before the main path dips and curves left. (If you go too far you will soon come up against a bridleway, with a gate on the left: in which case you must about turn and look for the correct path, which will then be on your left.)

Having set foot on the correct path you should follow it through the wood over a diagonal crossing-path and straight on to a stile overlooking a large field. Now it's a case of maintaining the same direction but across the field and aiming at the right-hand extremity of distant farm buildings – as indicated by a waymark arrow (260°). On the occasion of my first visit this field was high with wheat and the path not reinstated. If you have the same experience it would be right and proper to tread the correct route regardless, for you will be helping those who follow.

After crossing the field make your way to the right of the farm buildings and go over a stile leading into the garden of the farmhouse (waymarked and quite legal). There is soon another stile leading into a small paddock, after which it's half-left across the paddock to yet another stile and a lane.

Go right in the lane and follow it downhill to where it turns right. A rough track comes in from the left here and there's a fine view across the Thames from a field gate, including Lower Basildon and its church. You may also see the entrance gate to the National Trust's Basildon Park, and the rooftop of the house itself.

Stay in the lane until you meet some houses, then look for a track under trees on the left just before no. 2, the last double house. When this track opens out to more houses, turn left into a bridleway between Gattendon Lodge and Kingfisher Cottage. This bridleway is signposted to Whitchurch but we need it for 75 yards only – to a path on the right leading to a small 'permissive' footbridge. It's now a simple matter of following the Thames path back to Goring; a very pleasant 1½ miles.

If you are set on reaching the John Barleycorn without delay you could more quickly arrive there by turning right across a seated grassy area as soon as Goring Bridge comes into view. This will take you past a fenced brick building into Ferry Lane, which led to a river crossing before Goring Bridge was first built, and thence to the inn.

Bus Company Addresses

(and phone numbers for timetable enquiries).

Routes 27 and 61:
Aylesbury Bus, Smeaton Close, Brunel Park, Aylesbury,
Bucks HP19 3SU.
Aylesbury (0296) 23445.

Route 43/245:
Luton and District, Castle Street, Luton, Beds LU1 3AJ.
Luton (0582) 404074.

Route 252:
Hemel Bus, Two Waters Bus Garage, London Road, Hemel
Hempstead, Herts HP3 9AA.
Hemel Hempstead (0442) 216934.

Routes 27/344-347, 323-324, 325/328-330:
Wycombe Bus Company, Newlands Bus Station, High Wycombe,
Bucks HP11 2JD.
High Wycombe (0494) 520941.

Routes 336-337, 372, 373:
Chiltern Bus, 380 West Wycombe Road, High Wycombe,
Bucks HP12 3AH.
High Wycombe (0494) 464647.

Route 390:
Thames Transit, Horspath Road, Oxford OX4 2RY.
Oxford (0865) 772250.